OFFICE DESIGN

OFFICE

PETER B. BRANDT, AIA

INTRODUCTION BY M. ARTHUR GENSLER, JR., FAIA

DESIGN

WHITNEY LIBRARY OF DESIGN
An imprint of Watson-Guptill Publications/New York

For Roslyn

Senior Editor: Roberto de Alba
Associate Editor: Carl D. Rosen
Designer: Bob Fillie, Graphiti Graphics
Production Manager: Ellen Greene

First published in 1992 by Whitney Library of Design,
an imprint of Watson-Guptill Publications,
a division of BPI Communications, Inc.,
1515 Broadway, New York, NY 10036

Library of Congress Cataloging-in-Publication Data
Brandt, Peter B.
Office design / Peter B. Brandt.
p. cm.
Includes index.
ISBN 0-8230-3343-0
1. Offices—United States—Design and construction.
2. Interior architecture—United States. 3. Office decoration—
United States. I. Title.
NA6232.B73 1992
725'.23—dc20   92-9635
                                     CIP

Manufactured in the United States of America

First printing, 1992

1 2 3 4 5 6 7 8 9 10/97 96 95 94 93 92

CONTENTS

FOREWORD

Office design is a process. For the architect and interior designer it begins with obtaining the commission and follows through the logical steps of site selection, programming, schematic design, design development, contract documentation, actual construction, and furnishings acquisition, and concludes with move-in and evaluation. It includes such management tasks as negotiating contracts, organizing the team, budgeting, and scheduling. Each step must be done well for the project to be a success.

This book is the result of more than twenty years of experience in the field of office design, most of them with Gensler and Associates, recognized as one of the premier architectural firms in the United States specializing in interior planning and design. These pages present a broad overview of the office design process as I learned and practiced it. Fundamental to this design process are several concepts that have guided me in the writing.

The first is that office design is based on common sense; it is a logical process. That which appears mysterious or complex is mostly jargon, tradition, or methodology, developed to meet a particular problem or suit the needs of an individual architect or interior designer. *Rentable area*, for example, is simply a marketing strategy and *task lighting* nothing more than an updated version of the old-fashioned table lamp.

The second concept is that offices are for people. These people are not in the office to relax or be entertained. Office design is not the place for the latest stylistic trends; it is the place for real solutions to the real problems of human productivity and comfort.

The third concept is that there is never only one way, not even a "right" way or "better" way, to do anything in the interior planning and design of offices. Every client, every company, is different. Each has its own way of operating, its own corporate culture, and each is convinced that it is right.

Successful office design is not created by imposing old solutions but by asking questions, by working through a process of discovery with each client to determine the most appropriate answer in each case.

Successful projects have many characteristics in common. First, the client's needs and expectations are satisfied. The project is well and creatively designed. Costs and schedules are kept under control. Management and documentation is performed competently. The project team is experienced, committed, and enthusiastic. Finally, the professional fees are fair and the design firm makes a profit. The purpose of this book is to help make this happen.

I have avoided making a distinction between architect and interior designer. As this is being written, the questions of definition and scope of services are being hotly debated between the two professions. I have worked with members of both professions who were fully competent in all phases of interior planning and design. Although there are legal restrictions in different localities concerning who may do what, in this book they are treated equally.

The illustrations are deliberate simplifications meant to emphasize important concepts. On a real project, they would undoubtedly be more complex.

Many people have assisted me in the writing of this book. First, thanks to Arthur Gensler, my friend and mentor for more than eighteen years, who contributed the introduction to this book. I would like to thank my friends Dan Mac-Eachron, Andrew Suss, and Walter Thomas and my colleagues Robin Klehr Avia, Francisco Laurier, Diane Rupp, Deborah Taylor, and Chris Nims for their helpful comments. Thanks also to my students at the New York School of Interior Design. Finally, in my search for the most dedicated and knowledgeable critic I could find, I needed to go no further than my breakfast table. My wife, Roslyn, read every word. I knew that if she liked the book, I must be doing something right.

INTRODUCTION

BY M. ARTHUR GENSLER, JR., FAIA

Back in 1965, when I first began Gensler and Associates, an office facility was thought of as just another segment of a company's operational budget. Offices were often laid out by an office manager with graph paper and a Number 2 pencil. These concepts are no longer practical in today's business environment. Sophisticated programming and design techniques have been developed to ensure that the modern office is the most productive possible.

The age of information has replaced the industrial age. To compete successfully in today's markets, a company must truly be an information-based business, and it must also embrace technology to increase individual productivity and quality. Therefore, white-collar workers constitute over half of today's workforce, and most of them work in office environments. More time is spent in the office than anywhere else except the home.

In 1965 office facilities ranged from 3 to 10 percent of a corporation's assets. Today they are the largest item on a corporate balance sheet, representing about 25 percent of the total assets. Where facilities were once considered to be a fixed operational expense, they are now viewed as an ever-changing resource. It is recognized that a well-planned facility can be a significant factor in a company's attaining its strategic objectives. The well-designed office can increase productivity, help attract and keep quality employees, create a positive public image, and promote a strong corporate culture.

An office twenty-five years ago consisted of a bullpen of steel desks with manual typewriters. Today, the office is a complex unit of workstations and private offices, accommodating computers and sophisticated communications equipment. The desk has been replaced by a systems workstation that houses various heights of work surfaces, storage, communications, wiring, and lighting. With the dramatic rise in office rent, office facilities are now seriously regarded as a corporate asset and must be planned and maintained as such. Businesses recognize that quality office design is a good investment that positively affects productivity.

While the design process and financial value of office design have evolved over the past twenty-five years, a significant change has also taken place in the clients with whom we work. Clients have become more knowledgeable about the importance of appropriate design and expect a higher level of outstanding service and creative, responsive design. Architects and interior designers must work closely with clients to gain a true understanding of their businesses, to actively support their strategic plans, and to help them increase their productivity and image. Every client has to respond to a specific niche in today's market, and as such requires tailored services, not just off-the-shelf approaches.

The function of architects and interior designers is also undergoing change, and they are taking a more active role in assisting facilities managers in the planning and implementation of office facilities. Some design professionals have lost credibility because they lack knowledge of cost, schedules, and the true function of an office. They also have decreased ability to manage and control the process because of their mounting concerns with the escalating problem of liability. However, the truly professional architects and interior designers have emerged as team leaders in executing the office environments that are needed for today's successful businesses. These professionals are regaining the leadership role through their increased technical competence and their serious attention to office organization and productivity; issues that the client is demanding that they understand and address.

This book leads the architect and interior designer through the step-by-step phases and processes that occur on a typical office design project. I worked with Peter Brandt for over eighteen years at Gensler and Associates, where he developed those programs and systems that must be integrated into a successful project. Peter is a teacher and is an acknowledged leader in our field, and in this book he shares his expertise in various approaches to the design process. Twelve years ago, Peter and I coauthored *A Rational Approach to Office Design*, an American Management Association book. This new book takes the concepts that we explored there and explains them in detail, giving the reader the proper tools and necessary information to ensure an efficient project process and a successful result. It is worthwhile reading for both new designers and experienced professionals who must work in the world of today's business.

CHAPTER ONE

MARKETING

Success in architecture or interior design depends on many things, not the least of which is a love for the work and the competence to carry it out. Success may also depend on setting goals and taking steps to achieve them. While many architects and interior designers follow wherever opportunity leads, others try to plan their future in a more organized way. They state their goals in a *mission statement* and outline the path in a *business plan*.

The mission statement is a declaration of purpose and reflects the desires and interests of the principals of the design firm. It defines the firm's philosophy and the position the firm would like to fulfill in society and the marketplace. It guides the firm's attitude toward design, growth, personnel, professional service, and profitability.

The road map of the mission statement is the business plan. Working from the ideals of the mission statement, the business plan sets out a series of specific goals and objectives to be accomplished within a specific time period, usually from one to five years.

Mission statements and business plans explore every area of practice. There may be financial targets involving levels of sales, profitability, or market share. There may be aspirations for recognition by design awards, honors, or election to office in a professional organization. Goals may be established regarding numbers of employees and geographical spread. Finally, there may be a desire to help humankind or to advance the state of the art.

Central to the goal implementation process is the definition of the kind of work the firm would like to do. Although many architects and interior designers prefer the variety of a general practice, others are finding that the complexities of modern project types demand increasing levels of specialization. Office design is one of these fields. From being an afterthought tacked on to base building design services forty years ago, office design has grown to become the foundation specialty of significant numbers of design professionals. In the 1991 survey by *Interior Design* magazine, two-thirds of the "100 Interior Design Giants" listed office design as the major focus of their practice.

Like other fields of specialization, office design has its own traditions, knowledge base, and procedures. It requires a level of interest, experience, and commitment on the part of the principals of the firm to be successful. In choosing to provide office design services, architects and interior designers should first believe that that is what interests them, that they can be successful, that they can make a contribution to the community, and that they will have fun. After this is determined, the financial aspects should be considered. Expectation of financial reward alone is rarely a sufficient reason to practice a specialty. A design professional whose heart is in base building or residential design will not be happy doing offices, no matter how profitable.

Many architects and interior designers perform office design services successfully as part of a general practice. This can be accomplished only when the design professional recognizes and appreciates the special characteristics of office design and strives to master them. Office design is less successful when it is treated as a minor additional service to a base building design project. Firms specializing in high-rise office building design have generally found that it is not advisable to continue the design into the interior with the base building team. A separate team or department is required whose interests and talents are focused on office interiors. Many have also found that the interior design "tail" can end up wagging the base building "dog."

Many characteristics distinguish office design from other specialized areas of architecture and interior design:

❏ As with interior design projects generally, there is proportionately more time spent with the client than in traditional architectural practice. Clients are involved in design decisions in much greater detail. There are committees evaluating design, facility managers monitor-

ing budgets and schedules, and users examining the placement of every chair and copy machine. Therefore, a love of people and skill at working with them is a prerequisite of office design.

❏ It is necessary to master a large body of specialized knowledge about interior construction and furnishings. The contract office furniture industry is large and diversified, and just keeping up with new products takes significant time. Product libraries in design firms specializing in office design are generally two to three times the size of libraries in more traditional architectural firms.

❏ Office design requires an understanding of real estate and finance. Office design projects usually must meet strict bottom-line financial goals, and the interrelationships between rents, lease incentives, and construction and furnishings costs can be complicated.

❏ Some will find the aesthetic opportunities limited; the flights of fancy possible in store or restaurant projects are seldom appropriate for office design. Three-dimensional expression may be limited by the consistent ceiling height in most office space. There is, however, a seriousness of purpose, a programmatic and aesthetic logic, and an intellectual rigor that many architects and interior designers find challenging and conducive to design excellence.

PROJECT MARKETING

The function of marketing is to identify new business opportunities and to obtain design commissions. Marketing has two components: *business development* and *sales*. Business development is the planning process; establishing the reputation and credibility of the firm in the community and positioning the firm to be able to respond to opportunities. Sales is the process of seeking and being selected for a specific project.

The *marketing plan* is a written program used to identify and organize business development activities. By providing defined and realistic targets, a marketing plan provides an outline for action and encouragement for achievement, and it helps prevent wasted effort. Elements of a marketing plan include setting goals and objectives, assigning tasks, assessing strengths and weaknesses, developing marketing materials, implementing a public relations program, and finding and tracking potential clients.

Marketing Goals and Objectives

Marketing activity supports the firm's business plan. Many of the goals and objectives stated in the business plan are fleshed out in the marketing plan. These include financial goals, identification of geographic territory, an assessment of the strengths and weaknesses of the firm and its competition, and the definition of the firm's unique selling position.

Financial goals for marketing are generally stated in terms of fees generated per year from new projects. Through an analysis of past fee history and reference to a desired growth rate, a dollar-amount goal can be established.

Geographical goals define the communities or regions where the firm would like to concentrate its practice. They keep the firm from spreading itself too thinly and from wasting effort on projects that are outside of its natural territory, where chances of success are slim.

Identifying a geographical area for practice depends on a firm's perception of its ability to adequately service a given market. This may be the result of firm size and degree of specialization. A large firm specializing in stock brokerage or law firm projects will cover a wider geographic area than a small firm doing general office design. The identification of geographic spread helps to determine the viability of prospective projects and to efficiently concentrate marketing efforts.

A useful but sometimes painful exercise in the development of the marketing plan is the analysis of the strengths and weaknesses of both the firm and the competition. This must be done as candidly as possible and include an evaluation of design excellence, service quality, staff capability, technical expertise, management ability, and marketing skill. This will identify areas where the firm excels, as well as where steps must be taken to correct deficiencies. It will identify those qualities that set the firm apart from the competition.

Each design firm brings a different emphasis, with different priorities, to its approach to office design. One may emphasize technical competence, another its design creativity, and a third its attention to service. Each firm's special emphasis defines that firm's *unique selling position*—that niche in the marketplace that the firm is best qualified to fill. Once identified, marketing activities are directed to finding and servicing that niche.

A marketing plan should identify roles and responsibilities of firm members. To lead the marketing effort a major commitment is required from at least one of the principals. Marketing is most successful when it involves everyone in the firm, not just a few senior personnel. Whether assembling marketing materials, calling on new prospects, making presentations, or maintaining existing client relationships to assure return business, each firm member should be assigned those marketing tasks that he or she is best able to fulfill. When staff members are included, they develop a commitment to the firm and an involvement with its future. The results obtained are often surprising.

Bonuses or "commissions" for obtaining new work should be avoided. Marketing should be treated as simply another professional activity like designing, managing, or drafting. To treat it otherwise may cause resentment among staff personnel and imply an unwarranted importance to marketing. For all its visibility, marketing is basically a support activity to the primary business of the firm, which is to produce successful projects.

Marketing takes money, whether in the form of cash outlays for materials or in the form of time. A marketing budget can help to keep these costs realistic. A reasonable marketing budget may be in the range of 5 to 10 percent of net fees.

Marketing Materials

An important responsibility in a design firm is the management of *marketing files* and *resource materials*. This position may be filled by a principal, an administrative staff member, or a full-time marketing manager. Marketing materials must be accurate, timely, and readily available. Included among marketing materials are client mailing and reference lists, prospect address lists, brochure material, project case histories, slides, and photographs.

It is common for prospective clients to ask for a list of *references* of past clients for projects similar in type and scope to the one they propose. The list should include names, titles, addresses, and telephone numbers along with the type, size, location, and other project information. It should be kept current, and care should be taken that the information is accurate, including the spelling of names and correct titles. Individuals listed may be the

CEO, primary client contact, facility manager, or another person who would appear credible as a reference.

Reference lists should be relatively short with past clients carefully selected on the basis of their willingness to give a good report on the firm. References should always be contacted for permission to use their name and project data. Cost and fee information, in particular, should only be used with permission.

Every design firm should maintain a current *mailing list*, preferably in the form of a relational data base with the ability to sort information by subject. This list may include past clients, industry acquaintances, business development contacts, colleagues, and friends. Once again, care should be taken with correct spelling and correct titles. This list will be used for mailings of promotional materials, holiday greetings, announcements, and many other purposes.

Good projects should have good *photographs*. Design firms should hire the best photographer available; poor photographs are of no use in business development or public relations. Clients must be asked for permission for any photography, and requests that certain areas not be photographed or other requests for confidentiality must be respected. Many clients are willing to pay for or to share in the cost of photography, as they often have their own uses for the photographs. Some design firms include a paragraph in their design contracts specifically allowing for professional project photography.

Design firms are expected to produce and use excellent *graphics* in everything they do, from stationery to office forms to business development brochures. As an important and highly visible aspect of design, the firm's graphic image is reflective of the care and attention to detail the design firm brings to its project work.

Good graphics does not end with printed material. The organization and typing format of letters, proposals, and reports deserve equal care.

A firm's *brochure* is a primary marketing tool. This may be a bound volume or a loose-leaf presentation kit in a variety of formats. The bound volume may have an appearance of permanence but usually cannot be tailored to the specific needs of the project at hand. A loose-leaf format is more flexible; reprints and proposals can be integrated into a graphically attractive and coordinated presentation.

Another option for the brochure is videotape. Some firms now present their capabilities via television.

Public Relations

The function of *public relations* is to position the firm as a responsible and competent member of the community. Public relations activities include joining community organizations, giving speeches, holding seminars and teaching, issuing publications, and having office receptions. Many of these activities are pursued for personal, nonprofessional reasons. Marketing benefits are often simply the icing on the cake.

Business clubs and cultural organizations are a traditional American way to develop and maintain contacts with potential clients within the community. Organizations such as Chambers of Commerce and building-owner, real estate, construction, and facility management groups may provide opportunities to get to know specific target audiences. Often of particular interest to architects and interior designers are groups with a concern for aesthetics and the environment, such as landmarks or historical preservation committees, art museums, or design review boards. Professional organizations such as the American Insti-

tute of Architects (AIA), the American Society of Interior Designers (ASID), and the Institute of Business Designers (IBD) provide opportunities to keep current with the latest trends in the professions. Design firm staff members should be encouraged to actively participate in such groups, and firms are often willing to pay membership dues or other costs.

Speeches, seminars, and teaching offer occasions for architects and interior designers to fulfill civic responsibilities as well as maintain business development contacts. Civic groups and real estate, construction, and furnishings industry organizations frequently need speakers or seminar participants with specialized knowledge.

Many design firms have found that a newsletter is an excellent way to maintain contacts with past clients and to develop a file of material for marketing to new clients. As befits a firm promoting good design, the newsletter, typically four to eight pages long and issued quarterly, should be graphically excellent and handsomely printed. Newsletters generally feature pictures and descriptions of the firm's current projects. To make the newsletter of more lasting value, technical information that has real, practical use to the recipient may be included.

Receptions in the design firm's offices for existing and past clients, industry friends, and even competitors are a good way to renew old acquaintances, introduce the office staff, and let past clients know what the firm has been doing. Some firms have found that their reception areas and corridors make excellent art galleries for local artists or for specialized exhibitions that change several times a year. The opening of each new installation provides a good excuse for a party.

Publication is desirable both for current publicity and the long-term value from reprints. The architectural and interior design press is always looking for worthy projects to publish. Projects must, of course, be well designed, but beyond that, they must be excellently photographed to be considered. Once a project is published, reprints may be ordered for use in business development. Technical articles and essays about current issues within the professions are other ways architects and interior designers can see their names in print.

Finding Potential Projects

The heart of business development is *target market research*, which is the identification and tracking of potential clients. Sources of information include newspapers and other publications, past clients, and real estate and industry contacts.

Newspapers and technical magazines are good sources of information, primarily for obtaining a general feel for the market rather than specific project information, since by the time projects appear in print a design firm has generally already been selected. For federal government projects, the publication through which all federal agencies solicit design services is the *Commerce Business Daily*.

Architects and interior designers should be aware of new buildings being planned or under construction and companies that are planning to relocate. Developers, contractors, and real estate agents are excellent sources for identifying these potential clients. Building owners and real estate agents are in a good position to recommend design firms to tenants in their buildings.

The single best source for new work is past clients. If a design firm provided good service on an earlier project, they stand a good chance of being selected for the next one. Beyond this are the networks that exist within client groups. Lawyers, accountants, bankers, and stock brokers talk to each other. They know when their peers are planning to move, and they are in a position to give powerful recommendations. This, however, is not automatic. Assuming a past client was satisfied, contact should be maintained and the client regularly approached for information and recommendations.

SALES

Once identified, potential clients need to be approached. Usually an introduction can be arranged by a mutual acquaintance. If not, a *cold call* may be necessary. These are usually expected and well received by organizations planning new projects.

A cold call is not a sales pitch. Generally directed to the facility manager, it is a request for information about the scope and character of the project, for identification of the proper contact within the prospect's organization, and for the steps to be taken to be considered for the project. The sales effort really begins with the *follow-up letter*. Starting with a thank-you for the information given on the telephone, the letter may continue with a short description of the firm and its particular qualifications for the project in question. A brochure or other marketing material may be included.

To insure that prospective clients are contacted and that appropriate follow-up is done, a *marketing status report* may be used. This lists the project, the client contact and telephone number, the in-house contact, and the next action to be taken. The report might also include a rating code indicating the probability of receiving the commission.

The marketing status report should be reviewed and updated at weekly marketing meetings of principals, other senior

MARKETING STATUS REPORT

Date: April 12, 19—

Rating	Project	Prospect Contact	In-house Contact	Action
C	Tyrell Corporation, Los Angeles Ops. Center 76,000 sf	J. S. Sebastian 213–555–7654	RS	Discuss services 4/23/—
A	Federal Broadcasting Company, Cleveland Records Dept. remodeling 2,600 sf	Bunny Watson, director 216–555–9876	WL	Submit proposal 5/3/—
A	Law offices, London 40,000 sf	Sir Wilfred Robards, barrister 071–555–6543	BW	Present firm 4/27/—
C	Beautee Soap, Denver headquarters 140,000 sf	Evan Evans, president 303–555–2345	JC	Submit proposal 4/30/—
B	Kimberly Advertising, San Francisco regional office 95,000 sf	Kim Kimberley, president 414–555–6754	JC	Present firm 5/20/—
A	New York Inquirer, editorial offices, 26,000 sf	Jeremy Bernstein, General Manager	OW	Preliminary meeting 6/4/—

Page 1

MARKETING REPORT. This report should be reviewed and updated weekly. The rating code reflects an evaluation of the likelihood of receiving the commission for the listed project.

personnel, and the marketing staff. These meetings need not be long. Marketing activities are reviewed, new opportunities discussed, and assignments made. This is an excellent way to hold individuals accountable for maintaining contacts and producing results.

Effective sales involves learning as much as possible about the client and the project. Visits to the company's existing facilities can usually be arranged. A company's annual report, sales brochures, and promotional literature often reveal much about corporate culture and image. Financial information is available from Dun & Bradstreet as well as from the annual report.

Research should be done on individuals in the target company—this includes, for example, learning what organizations they belong to, what boards they sit on, what outside interests they have. Information about executives is usually available from industry and professional directories, as well as *Who's Who*. Common ground is often found that can serve as an opening for an introduction.

The best source for project information is the prospective client. They expect architects and interior designers to ask questions and are usually more than willing to provide information about the type, size, location, budget, and schedule of their project. Other appropriate questions for a prospective client include how and when will the design firm be selected, who will sit on the selection committee, and what other firms are being considered for the commission.

More and more organizations are insisting that vendors of all sorts, including architects and interior designers, understand their business as a prerequisite for using their products or services. Solid general knowledge about the prospective client's field of endeavor is both flattering and lends great credibility to the message of the design firm. Architects and interior designers with a detailed understanding of banking, law, accounting, manufacturing, or insurance will have an advantage with clients in those fields. Much of this information is gained from the experience of having completed projects of similar scope in the same field. Much can also be learned by reading books and professional journals. While architects and interior designers cannot be expected to have in-depth knowledge of all of the technical intricacies of all of their clients, they should certainly know enough to be able to intelligently discuss clients' concerns in their own language.

The Sales Presentation

An effective sales presentation must be well prepared and rehearsed. All of the facts and logistics must be in place, including the date, time, length of presentation, and location. If many firms are presenting there may be a choice of presentation times. Some architects and interior designers prefer to be first, a situation in which they assume the responsibility for orienting the audience to the project process as well as presenting the capabilities of their own firm. They believe that establishing the benchmark against which others are judged gives them an edge. Others like to be last, so that they can concentrate their presentation on critical questions after routine issues have been dealt with in earlier presentations. They look forward to closing with a bang.

The prospective client should be asked how many people will attend the presentation and their names and titles. This is done so that the correct number of brochures or other material may be prepared and, if the presentation is to be held in the design firm's offices, that the room size is adequate, the correct number of chairs are available, and adequate food or refreshments are provided.

There is no single right way to structure a presentation—it is a matter of style and comfort. Some marketers like to use photo brochures, slides, or video presentations; others feel more comfortable presenting verbally; most use some combination of the two. However structured, a presentation must be carefully organized to achieve the specific end of the firm's being selected for the project.

The characteristics of a successful presenter are a reflection of the qualities of the whole person. Nice people **do** finish first. Presentation skills are the technique of demonstrating these qualities successfully. These techniques can be learned. A charismatic personality is certainly advantageous, but even the best natural marketers work hard at maintaining their skill.

Effective marketers are enthusiastic, and their enthusiasm is infectious. They are confident in the ability of their firm to accomplish the project. They exude energy. They are well prepared, knowledgeable, competent, and thorough. They exhibit a genuine interest in the client and his or her concerns, and they have the ability to listen.

Skill at presentation is the ability to put nervousness, shyness, and uncertainty aside so that they do not obscure the message to be delivered. Presentation skill can be mastered through preparation and practice.

Every design firm member who will attend the presentation must be given a specific part to play. People who attend but do not participate are suspect. At least one day before the presentation, it should be rehearsed. Many firms videotape these rehearsals to help improve presentation techniques.

Upon arrival at a presentation, introductions are customary. One member of the presentation team should be responsible for obtaining the correct name, title, address, and telephone number of each client representative, usually by asking for business cards. This is important: Clients interpret misspellings and incorrect titles in follow-up correspondence as an indication of carelessness and lack of interest.

A typical project presentation might begin with a short introduction and welcome from the design firm principal. This may be followed by a short history of the firm emphasizing design philosophy and relevant experience, then a slide presentation of projects similar to that proposed, and finally a discussion of the proposed project and the design firm's scope of services, design approach, and methodology for implementation. Emphasis should be placed on the design firm's unique qualities as they relate to the prospect's specific needs. The last few minutes might be left for questions closing with thanks and a recapitulation concerning why the firm should be selected.

Immediately following the presentation, a thank-you letter should be written to all the client participants from the senior design firm representative thanking them for their consideration. This is also an opportunity to provide any further information requested, to emphasize the firm's qualifications, and to mention the inevitable points that were only remembered five minutes after the end of the presentation.

Proposals

The natural follow-up to a presentation is a *proposal for services*. Many clients send formal requests for proposals (RFP) with detailed itemized questions. These are best answered in exactly the format requested, although suitable embellishment is encouraged.

The federal government has formalized the proposal process with its Standard Forms 254 and 255. Form 254 is an overview of the firm's qualifications and experience over a five-year period. This form should be updated annually and sent to those state, city, or federal agencies that may have projects of interest to the design firm. Standard Form 255 is a project-specific response, sent in answer to an announcement in the *Commerce Business Daily*. The basic forms are fairly short and ask statistical questions about disciplines provided, staff capabilities, and project experience. Firms specializing in government projects, however, have turned the production of these forms into high art—computerized, professionally printed, and expanded to several hundred pages with photographs and other elaboration.

Whether or not the form of response to an RFP is specified by the client, a proposal should be graphically attractive, informative, and specific about the firm's qualifications as the best choice for the project. The same elements that were important in the marketing presentation are equally important here—history and philosophy of the firm, staff qualifications, relevant experience, proposed services, methodology for accomplishment, and a list of references. If a fee quotation is requested it should be provided. When fees are quoted, the scope of services should be quite specific about what is and what is not included, even to the extent of including a proposed form of contract.

Specific design solutions to the client's problem should not be attempted as part of marketing presentations or proposals. Ethics aside, a responsible solution to an office design problem is the result of a detailed study of the client's requirements, not a glib scheme based on superficial preliminary information. The design is the end of the process, not the beginning.

The final step in marketing is *feedback and evaluation*. For both projects won and projects lost, the clients should be asked for a debriefing. They will generally be quite candid and helpful in a positive way. The knowledge of why a firm was or was not selected—what it did wrong as well as what it did right—can be invaluable in preparing for the next sales presentation or proposal.

The success of a design firm depends on the quality of its product, personnel, and procedures. In the long run, if the quality isn't there, marketing will not create it. Although elaborate business development and clever sales techniques may fool some of the people some of the time, ultimately, no amount of marketing will help a firm that cannot produce. Without effective marketing, however, the firm may never get the opportunity to prove itself.

CHAPTER TWO

PROFESSIONAL
SERVICE CONTRACTS

After an architect or interior designer has been selected for a project, but before work can actually begin, a contract must be executed between the design professional and the client, most likely the owner or tenant of the new office space. In a *professional service contract* the design professional agrees to perform a specific scope of work, such as project design, documentation, or management. In return the client agrees to pay a defined fee.

A professional service contract is for service only; no goods, products, or physical construction are involved. These are covered by other types of agreements such as a *general contract* for construction or *purchase orders* for furniture, furnishings, and equipment (FF&E). For these types of contracts, compensation is determined by the value of goods provided.

The distinction between the providers of professional service, such as architects, interior designers, and engineers, and the providers of goods, such as contractors, vendors, and manufacturers, is often clouded. Traditionally interior designers combined the two, while architects avoided providing anything other than strictly professional service. Today, while most design professionals provide professional services only for office design projects, both architects and interior designers may sometimes act as furnishings dealers or take ownership positions in projects.

On the other side of the coin, general contractors have begun to offer construction management services and dealers have begun to offer furnishings project management services, both with professional service fee arrangements.

Where contracts for service appear to overlap with contracts for goods, there may be a concern about potential conflicts of interest. Different rules and regulations apply to contracts for goods, such as the Uniform Commercial Code for furniture sales. From the legal and insurance aspect, warranties are different. Professional liability differs greatly from strict product liability. Finally there are the ethical concerns of various professional organizations. When both goods and services are provided by the same firm or company, they should be kept contractually distinct. Architects and interior designers should not appear to be receiving both a design fee and a sales commission for the same increment of work.

FORMS OF CONTRACT

A contract has many practical uses. One is the prevention of misunderstandings by defining, in language understood by both parties, exactly what is to be provided for exactly what compensation. A well-written contract clarifies and strengthens a relationship between the design professional and the client. This is particularly true in the field of architecture and interior design, where many of the terms, procedures, and processes are unfamiliar to the layperson.

Another purpose of a contract is damage control. A well-written contract contains terms and conditions to fairly protect both parties when something goes wrong. Professional service is by nature highly subjective and no written contract can adequately cover every contingency. While it is no substitute for a good client relationship, a contract can provide a safety net if the client relationship deteriorates.

The simplest type of contract is a verbal agreement, which may be legally binding under certain circumstances. The virtues of its simplicity and appearance of absolute trust are generally outweighed by the potential danger to both the design professional and the client. Where the slightest possibility for misunderstanding exists, a verbal contract should not be used.

A second form of contract may be a letter to the client, often as short as a single page. A *letter contract* contains a description of the work to be done, the fee to be paid, and the terms and conditions of the agreement. A signature line is provided for client acceptance.

Letter contracts are by nature informal, and this may cause problems. Because of the informality, important points may be forgotten or missed in the writing of the letter. The letter may lack enough objectivity, force, and formality to provide an effective vehicle to solve serious disagreements between the parties. For these reasons letter contracts are generally used for smaller projects with knowledgeable clients who understand the design process, for additions or modifications to existing agreements, or with clients with whom a professional relationship has been previously established.

The formal written contract generally provides the soundest basis for furnishing design services. The most common format for these agreements are standard forms such as document B171, available from the American Institute of Architects (AIA) and the American Society of Interior Designers (ASID), titled "Standard Form of Agreement for Interior Design Services." These organizations also provide a document B177, "Abbreviated Form of Agreement for Interior Design Services," for smaller projects, projects of limited scope, or when interior planning and design services are an additional service to a base building design contract.

Among the merits of AIA and ASID standard forms is the integration with other documents used in construction and furnishings. Contract administration duties described in these contracts, for example, mesh with those outlined in standard general conditions. When standard design service contracts are modified, corresponding revisions should be made to other documents.

Many large design firms have developed their own forms of contract, worked out with their attorneys and reflecting years of experience. Some clients, particularly those with sophisticated facilities departments, have developed forms of contract that they require be used by their consultants. Contracts presented by these clients should be carefully reviewed, preferably with the assistance of an attorney.

KANE & LELAND/185 West 74th St/New York NY 10023/212–555–1941

May 3, 19—

Ms. Bunny Watson, Director of Research
FEDERAL BROADCASTING COMPANY
10543 Euclid Boulevard
Cleveland, Ohio 45060

Dear Ms. Watson,

I enjoyed meeting with you last Thursday to discuss the proposed remodeling of your records department. We are pleased you have selected us for this project.

We understand that the scope of our work will include architectural and interior design services for a new library, office, and work areas of approximately 2,600 rentable square feet. We will meet with you and your staff to discuss detailed requirements, prepare space plans and designs for your approval, prepare construction and furnishings documents, and make a maximum of four site visits to observe construction. We will coordinate our work with that of your mechanical and electrical engineers. We expect all work will be completed by October 31, 19—.

All work will be performed on an hourly basis at our standard flat rates. Total fees will not exceed $27,500. We will bill you for normal out-of-pocket expenses at cost plus 10 percent.

If you agree, please sign and return a copy of this letter. We look forward to working with Federal Broadcasting once again.

Very truly yours,
KANE & LELAND/ARCHITECTS

Jedidiah Leland, Principal

Accepted by: _____ Date: _____

LETTER FORM CONTRACT. This format should only be used for projects of limited scope or for small projects with clients with whom one has an established working relationship.

Some clients may object to the standard AIA and ASID agreements as being too "slanted" toward the design professional, particularly in the areas of responsibility during contract administration, professional liability, and ownership of documents. They may request revisions to the standard wording.

The services of an attorney are advisable for most formal contracts, particularly contracts for very large or complex projects, for extensive revisions to standard form contracts, and for client-supplied contracts. The professional liability insurance carrier may be consulted as well.

A contract's usefulness is wasted if it is not fully understood. A disadvantage of long, complicated contracts, full of "fine print" and legal phraseology, concepts, and procedures, is that they may not be carefully read by the parties to the agreement and may not accurately reflect the specific needs of the project at hand. When a problem arises, the design firm may find, to its chagrin, that the detailed contract wording does not agree with what it had in mind.

Another problem is that professional service is inherently highly subjective and no contract can cover every contingency. When carried to an extreme, literal reliance on contract language can harm rather than help a relationship. Even the strictest contract must carry within it the flexibility to respond to the practical needs of the project.

CONTRACT CONTENT

To the extent that every project and every client is different, no two contracts for interior planning and design services will be the same. Certain details will vary in each separate document. Even when using a standard AIA or ASID form, modifications may be necessary to match the contract with the needs of the project.

There are, however, essential elements that will be present in one form or another in every contract. These include project identification, a scope of basic services, a description of additional services, the client's responsibilities, a time schedule, a method of compensation, terms and conditions, and an acceptance block.

Project Identification

The first section of a formal written contract is devoted to the facts about the project. These will generally include the date of contract execution, name and address of the client, the name and location of the project, and the name and address of the design firm. Other consultants expected to be associated with the project may be included for reference.

The project identification should also include a brief description of the type of project, whether general office space, executive office space, computer center, food service facility, and so forth. It should include a brief description of the type of service to be performed, such as full interior planning and design services, space planning only, or construction documents only. It should also include the approximate size of each type of space in the project. The reason for these descriptions is that they are generally the basis for setting fees. Should any of these change significantly, such as a computer center increasing from 10,000 to 100,000 square feet or general office areas being replaced by executive offices, the scope of work may be seriously affected and there may be justification for a revision to the fee amount or fee basis.

These descriptions do not replace the more accurate program requirements and area calculations covered in other sections of the contract. Their purpose here is to act as "triggers" when major scope changes occur.

Scope of Basic Services

The scope of basic services section of the professional service contract should state exactly what is expected of the design firm in approximately the order in which the services will be performed. The level of detail and precision used in describing the scope of basic services depends on the type of fee arrangement, the relative "tightness" of the fee, and the type of client. The scope must be described in enough detail to insure that the client gets satisfactory service and that the design professional gets an adequate fee, yet not be so restrictive as to inhibit the design process.

Fixed fee contracts generally demand a more precisely defined scope of services than contracts performed on an hourly basis. A fixed fee contract for a government agency, for example, may not only describe the scope of work in great detail, but may also specify the exact number of drawings of each type to be produced and the exact number of presentations to be made.

Some design professionals prefer that all contracts contain a limitation on the number of space plans, design presentations, and design development schemes to be prepared as part of basic services. They believe this encourages clients to make timely decisions. They are concerned by potential problems created by clients who seem never to be happy, who demand continual revisions in ever-increasing detail. They prefer contracts that state that if the client is not satisfied after two or three tries, additional schemes may be prepared as a supplemental service for additional fees.

Other architects and interior designers disagree, arguing that the design professional's basic obligation to produce acceptable design work cannot be limited to a specific number of schemes and that the bad feelings generated by asking for additional fees before satisfactory work has been produced is not the way to maintain a successful relationship. They believe that if excessive designs and presentations become necessary, a deeper problem exists, one that cannot be solved by reference to contractual language.

In the AIA and ASID standard contracts, basic services are divided into five phases: programming, schematic design, design development, contract documents, and contract administration. Each phase is then described in paragraphs as a series of sequential tasks concluding with approval of the phase by the client.

The importance of phases as an organizing structure for projects lies in the requirement of a formal, written approval of each phase before the next phase may begin. Often these approvals trigger fee requests and payments. These approvals force an evaluation and confirmation of the design firm/client relationship. Without such periodic review, problems can multiply, remaining below the surface until the end of the project, when they become unmanageable.

One way to bring clarity to the approval process is to define a set of *deliverables*, the work product that is to be formally presented to the client for written approval as the last step of each phase. The deliverable at the conclusion of the programming phase may be the program report; at the conclusion of schematic design, space plans and preliminary concept studies; at the conclusion of design development, "scope" documents and materials and finishes selections; and at the conclusion of the contract document phase, complete drawings and specifications for construction and furnishings.

Deliverables common to all phases are new or updated budgets and schedules.

These get progressively more detailed and more accurate as the project proceeds. They require the same review and approval procedure as drawings and designs.

While a five-phase division is typical, it is not mandatory. Phasing should follow the needs of the project. If feasibility studies or building selection or evaluation services are included in basic services, they should be added as a separate phase. If programming for the project has been done by others, this phase should be eliminated and a paragraph added to the schematic design phase to cover program review and evaluation. (A paragraph may also be added to the additional services section to cover revising the program for additional fees.) For small projects, schematic design and design development may be combined. Some design professionals like to define the bidding or negotiation of construction and furnishings contracts as a separate phase. However defined, each phase should have specific tasks that must be accomplished between a defined start and a defined finish.

Sometimes phases may overlap. On a large project each floor of the building may follow its own schedule of design and construction. The architect or interior designer may be space planning one floor while preparing construction documents for another. In this situation, it may be wise to divide the project into subprojects, each following its own scope of services track.

Additional Services

Additional or supplementary services are those services that the architect or interior designer may offer to the client that are not included in the basic services fee. If the client elects to use these services, the architect or interior designer should prepare an authorization stating exactly what services are to be provided and what the additional fee will be. Work should never begin until authorized in writing by the client.

Additional services may be listed in professional service contracts as a "shopping list" from which the client may pick and choose. Some of these services may be necessary for the project but may be initially intended to be performed by the client or other consultants. Services of this type might include feasibility studies; building evaluations or comparative building studies; engineering services; special studies for artwork, acoustics, lighting, records retention, security or communications; studies for subtenant spaces; and the preparation of record or as-built drawings.

A typical additional service is project representation at the site beyond that required for basic services. Fees for the contract administration phase of a project generally account for no more than 20 to 30 percent of the total design fee, and much of that is consumed by work performed in the design firm offices. For all but the largest projects, fees will not cover more than periodic site visits. Where there is any question concerning the time to be spent on the site performing basic service work, the number of hours or days per week should be stated in the contract.

While periodic visits are generally sufficient to observe the progress of construction and perform other basic service responsibilities, many clients want full-time design firm representation on site. This may constitute a legitimate additional service requiring specific client authorization. The authorization should state the duties, responsibilities, and limitations of the authority of the field representative, as well as the additional fees to be paid.

Custom design of individual private offices may be an additional service. When private office furnishings are standardized by job title for a project, their selection and specification is generally included as a basic service in the design contract. If, however, private office furnishings and finishes are individually chosen for a particular occupant, the basic service fee usually will not cover this work.

Changes in a project may require additional services. A change must fulfill two criteria before additional fees can be charged. First, it must be a change to work previously approved by the client—thus the necessity for obtaining written approvals at the end of each phase of the project. Second, the change must necessitate additional work by the design firm. If no additional work is required, it is difficult to justify additional fees even though a change may have occurred. Changes may include program revisions, changes to design concepts, materials or furnishings selections, or work required for change orders requested by contractors.

Change is a particularly sensitive issue since at some point in every project the program and design must be "frozen" in order for the project to be implemented. For a dynamic organization used to constantly adding and changing staff positions, this is often hard to understand.

Changes usually affect project budgets and schedules as well as fees. An analysis of these implications is often included in the additional service authorization.

Often additional services are made necessary by situations beyond the control of the architect or interior designer. These may include consideration of contractor-proposed alternates, work required by defaults or delays in contractors' work, additional work caused by strikes, fires, or project delays beyond the control of the design professional, revisions caused by new laws or building code revisions, or by failure of the client to make timely decisions.

Client's Responsibilities

In addition to paying the bills, there are other client responsibilities under a professional service contract. The architect or interior designer has a right to know if the client has the financial means to fulfill the contract and the client may be obligated to furnish proof. The client must supply the information required for programming and must give timely approvals when requested. Laboratory tests and inspections are the obligation of the client, as are legal, accounting, insurance, or auditing services necessary for the projects.

Some of the client's duties may not be so obvious. The client is typically required to supply an inventory of existing furnishings and new and existing office equipment to be used on the project. The equipment information is particularly important since it affects mechanical, electrical, and structural specifications. If the owner needs technical help in gathering this information, the architect, interior designer, or engineers may assist in this work as an additional service.

Another owner's obligation is the designation of a single individual to represent the owner in dealings with consultants. Usually many people in the client's organization have an interest in the project and without a single point of contact, chaos could result.

The owner is responsible for providing base building drawings, specifications, and other source documents that the architect or interior designer needs in order to proceed. These may not be readily available and the assistance of the design professional may be needed. This often occurs with older buildings when measured drawings may be required. This can pose a serious problem for the design firm. Measured drawings of existing construction are difficult and time consuming to produce, and errors inevitably creep in. The cost in fees to prepare measured drawings sufficient for the design professional to guarantee against *any* errors is usually prohibitive and not worth the effort. It is generally more cost effective for the design professional to prepare drawings using an ordinary level of care with the understanding that the client will pay for correcting problems in the field caused by minor errors in the measured drawings.

Typically, the client is responsible for preparing the initial project budget that is presented to the design professional during the programming phase. This budget is usually very general in nature, sometimes limited to nothing more than a statement of the total amount the client desires to spend for the project.

If the preparation of the initial budget is beyond the technical capabilities of the client, the architect or interior designer may be asked to assist in its preparation. This assistance does not relieve the client of responsibility for the budget. However, the design professional is responsible for advising the client as to the adequacy of the budget for the accomplishment of the project.

The client is responsible for filing the project with governing authorities and for paying construction permit fees. The design firm typically assists in the process as a basic service.

A common word that carries important meaning is the word *assist*. While most phrases in a contract connect performance of a task ("the architect shall prepare drawings...") with accountability

for that task, some work performed by the design professional is for the purpose of assisting a client in the fulfillment of an obligation for which the client may not be technically competent. Such tasks may include the preparation of an initial budget and the filing of documents with a building department. The responsibility of the design professional in these situations may be limited to an educational one; to insure that the client fully understands the procedure at hand.

Compensation

An accurate fee estimate requires an evaluation of the time and effort required to produce a project. There are many methods used to charge *fees* to clients, such as percentage of project cost, lump sum, cost plus a fee, hourly, or hourly to a defined maximum. Each has its advantages and disadvantages. Whichever method is chosen, however, a given scope of work will require a predictable amount of time. This translates directly into fee dollars by multiplying the hours worked times the *billing rate* of the person (or CADD terminal) doing the work. The calculation begins with the establishment of billing rates.

Billing rates are usually based on salary. Benefits, such as vacation time and hospitalization costs, that accrue to the individual are added to the employee's hourly salary to arrive at Direct Personnel Expense (DPE). The billing rate is then calculated by adding DPE to a prorated charge for office overhead and a factor for desired profit.

As a typical example, overhead of 125 percent of DPE, and a desired profit of 20 percent, result in a billing rate of approximately 2.75 x DPE.

DPE billing rates are often converted into flat hourly billing rates for management simplicity and as a negotiating strat-

FEE DETERMINATION WORKSHEET

Remodeling of the records department for Federal Broadcasting, Cleveland. Scope of work includes programming, schematic design, design development, construction and furnishings documents, and construction observation (4 trips) for approximately 2,600 rentable square feet. Project budget is $240,000.

Prepared by Jed Leland, April 31, 19—
Estimate of Personnel and Time Required

Programming—1 week

Principals	8 hrs. @ $150		$ 1,200
Project Manager/Designer	24	100	2,400
			3,600

Schematic Design/Design Development—3 weeks

Principals	4	150	600
Project Manager/Designer	48	100	4,800
			5,400

Construction and Furnishings Documents—4 weeks

Principals	4	150	600
Project Manager/Designer	64	100	6,400
Drafter	40	60	2,400
			9,400

Construction Observation—12 weeks

Principals	4	150	600
Project Manager/Designer	48	100	4,800
			6,600
Subtotal			25,000
Contingency—10%			2,500
Total Estimated Fee			$27,500

Project Budget	$240,000
Fee @ 10% of Project Budget	$24,000
Rentable Area	2,600
Fee @ $10.00 per Rentable Square Foot	$26,000

FEE DETERMINATION WORKSHEET. A simple format to assist in determining the appropriate fee for a project.

egy. Whereas the DPE multiplier is an obvious target for fee negotiation, flat rates give the appearance of permanence. Flat rates may be established by rounding off or making other appropriate adjustments to a calculated DPE billing rate.

In many firms computer costs are treated as overhead. If, however, computer-aided design and drafting (CADD) costs are to be billed on a project-by-project basis, billing rates need to be set. Hardware and software costs may be amortized to arrive at a cost per hour. Factors may be added for profit, downtime, or training to establish the billing rate.

Once billing rates are set, total hours for each team member for each phase are estimated based on the projected schedule for the project. These hours multiplied by each team member's billing rate gives the fee for the phase. Allowances should be made for administrative and management time. For projects lasting a year or more, fee projections may include allowances for periodic salary increases. The total for all phases plus a reasonable contingency gives the projected total required fee for the project.

The phases of basic services are the units of work usually used to estimate fees. They have defined scopes and specific durations, which make them easy to track. However, projects may also be broken down in other ways for fee-estimating purposes. Task lists, subprojects, subphases, or other defined elements of work may be equally useful in estimating fees.

It is usually unwise to divide the project too finely into subphases and tasks for purposes of fee calculation. Uncertainties and contingencies pile on top of one another and inaccuracies compound as the number of separate calculations increases.

At best a fee projection is an educated guess. To increase accuracy the calcula-tion should be validated in as many ways as possible. Others in the design firm might perform the fee calculation independently and have the results compared. The projection may be compared with actual fees spent for similar projects done in the past. Historical fees may be compared with projects by looking at fees per phase, fees per square foot, fees as a percentage of project cost, and, for construction documents, fees per drawing.

In addition to fees, design firms are entitled to reimbursement for out-of-pocket expenses that directly benefit the project. Typical reimbursable expenses include costs for reproduction of drawings and specifications, postage, long-distance telephone and facsimile costs, messenger-service costs, and costs of presentation and other materials purchased specifically for the project. Engineering fees and the fees of other subconsultants may be reimbursable, as are expenses for building permits and fees.

Travel in connection with the project is generally reimbursable, including living expenses and transportation costs for out-of-town travel. Costs for professional renderings, models, or mock-ups are generally reimbursable, although in-house study models and sketches are not.

If computer costs are not treated as overhead and not included in fees, they are often billed as reimbursable. Costs might include both actual computer drawing (CPU) time and plotting time. Clerical time for specification typing is often treated as reimbursable, as are costs for data processing.

If the client specifically requests additional professional liability insurance beyond what the design firm normally carries, the additional premiums may be reimbursable.

Some design firms bill reimbursable expenses at cost. Others mark up reimbursables by a reasonable percentage to cover administrative and carrying costs.

Invoices are normally submitted monthly. For fees on an hourly basis, actual hours and billing rates are shown and extended. When fees are on a fixed fee or percentage of cost basis, billings are based on the percent of work complete by phase and hours and billing rates are not applicable.

Unlike construction contracts where a percentage of each invoice is withheld pending project completion, payments for professional service are generally expected to be paid in full each month. Some design firms add a percentage service charge to fees not paid within a reasonable time.

Terms and Conditions

Every contract contains terms and conditions, sometimes called *boilerplate*, that govern the performance of the parties to the contract. These cover such issues as liability, insurance, indemnification, arbitration, and termination. Among the most problematic is the issue of ownership of documents.

A basic concept of professional service is that the client is paying for mental activity, not a product. In the case of architecture, interior design, and engineering, drawings and specifications are instruments of that activity. The client's rights are limited to the right to build from these drawings and specifications on one occasion. The design professional retains ownership of the documents.

This is recognized in law. Like books and artwork, technical drawings are "original works of authorship" covered by copyright laws. Legally, a client has no more right to a design professional's drawings than does the purchaser of a book to change the author's words or reprint the book without permission.

Many clients have difficulty with that concept, believing they are buying a product rather than a service. There are two practical consequences to this position. The first is fair compensation for the reuse of documents. Unlike drawings for motels or restaurants, however, which can be easily used over and over again, drawings and specifications for interior office space are generally only of use for one particular project. The exact combination of program and building configuration seldom repeats itself. In this situation architects and interior designers have little to fear that their drawings will be used again without payment.

The second consequence is far more serious. Like a medical diagnosis or legal opinion, construction and furnishings documents are intended to be implemented under the control of the author. If the design professional is dismissed or otherwise prohibited from exercising control over the use of documents, the professional liability consequences could be significant. New and unforeseen situations constantly arise during project implementation, and changes that would be simply handled by the design professional during the normal course of construction may become a cause for a major liability claim if the design professional is no longer around.

It is bad policy to give up ownership of documents. Design professionals should do so only after consulting with an attorney and their professional liability insurance carrier, and with the assurance that they are adequately protected from the consequences of unauthorized reuse of documents. At a minimum, architects and interior designers must be allowed to remove their names from the documents and be relieved of all liability once the professional service contract has been terminated.

Acceptance Block

The final section of a contract is the *acceptance block*. This contains the signatures of persons authorized to sign for both parties to the contract. If there is reluctance on the part of a client to sign a contract, this may signify a deeper problem requiring resolution before project work can begin.

Theoretically, no work should begin on the project until the contract has been fully executed. In practice there are often small points that take considerable time to resolve. In these cases a letter of intent may be sufficient to allow work to commence. Architects and interior designers should be aware, however, that beginning work without a fully executed contract may seriously diminish their negotiating position.

A signed contract should be a working reference throughout the project. Copies, perhaps edited to remove confidential fee information, should be reviewed and periodically referred to by the entire design team.

ENGINEERS AND OTHER CONSULTANTS

Few office projects can be designed and documented by architects or interior designers alone. Generally, other consultants are required to perform parts of the design or to perform other tasks that the move to new offices makes necessary or practical.

Consultants are selected with the same procedure as architects and interior designers. A scope of work is determined, proposals are solicited, interviews are conducted, and references checked. This procedure can be either rigorous or informal depending on the scope of work involved and the desires of the client or design professional.

Items to consider when selecting a consultant include proven ability in his or her particular field and a harmonious working relationship with the architect or interior designer. If aesthetic issues are involved, such as lighting or graphics, the consultant should have a design philosophy that complements that of the architect or interior designer. If both firms use CADD systems, they should be compatible.

Consultants may be retained by the architect or interior designer and their work included within the maximum fee quotation. This is frequently done with consultants with a full-service, ongoing role in the project, such as the mechanical engineer, electrical engineer, and food service consultant. The agreement between the design firm and the consultant should be on the same fee basis and closely parallel that between the client and design firm. Indemnification provisions should be equally broad. If a standard AIA form is being used between the client and the architect, the AIA document C141, "Standard Form of Agreement Between Architect and Engineer," is a related document that should be considered.

When consultants are hired directly by the design firm, they typically share the same risk of payment as the architect and interior designer and are asked not to expect payment until the design firm has been paid.

These consultants may also be retained by the client directly with the understanding that they work under the direction of the architect or interior designer. Although many design professionals feel that they lose control of the process when they do not directly retain the consultants, others feel that this is not an issue and that direct retention by the client makes accounting simpler, payment quicker, and clarifies liability issues.

Consultants whose work is part of the architect or interior designer's additional services may be retained based on a letter of agreement proposed by the consultant and approved by the client. This is common for lighting consultants, acoustical consultants, audio-visual consultants, graphics designers, artwork consultants, and others whose work is of a specialized, relatively short-term nature.

Consultants whose work consists of implementing the construction and furnishing of the project, such as construction managers and furniture project managers, are usually retained directly by the client. Contracts are typically in a form proposed by the consultant. One form of contract frequently used in construction management is AIA document B801, "Standard Form of Agreement Between Owner and Construction Manager." Architects and interior designers should review these contracts to see that they are compatible with their professional service agreement.

Clients may retain consultants whose work, although independent of that of the architect or interior designer, directly affects the project. Such consultants may include real estate advisors, program-mers, cost consultants, management consultants, telecommunications and computer engineers, security consultants, and relocation consultants, as well as attorneys, accountants, and insurance advisors. While they may not have access to the actual contracts, architects and interior designers should be aware of the scope of work in each of these agreements.

In new buildings the landlord often provides the services of consultants as part of the lease workletter. These may include mechanical, electrical, and structural engineers, as well as the services of the base building or tenant development architects who may be available to prepare construction documents. Services are described in the lease workletter and fees are invoiced to the tenant by the building management, who may add a percentage as a project management fee.

Building rules and regulations may affect the hiring of consultants. Landlords may insist on using the base building mechanical, electrical, and structural engineers or consultants selected from a list of those familiar with the building systems in order to maintain engineering continuity.

CHAPTER THREE

PROJECT
INITIATION

A goal of project management is to produce a project as efficiently as possible. In practice this means implementing procedures to allow maximum effort to be expended in programming, design, and production, while minimizing time spent in administration.

The development of efficient project procedures begins with an orientation period that begins as soon as the design contract has been signed. The design team and the client's project team are organized and get to know each other. Project goals are established. Policies and procedures are determined, and lines of communication are forged. In many ways this is the most important activity in the entire project, for the procedures and methods of implementation established at this point can set the tone and character of all the other work.

The *project organization* is the structure that defines the relationship between the individuals working on a project. This relationship may be described in a written outline of roles and responsibilities or may be graphically displayed in an organization chart. However stated, the project organization deserves careful thought. A successful project is a well-organized project. Conversely, if a project has problems, the first place to look is the organization chart.

A project organization may take any one of a variety of forms; there is no one right or best way. The type of client, the size and type of project, the talents of team members, and many other factors will influence the selection of the form of project organization. An entrepreneurial client may be best served by a different form of organization than a bureaucratic client. A project with strong design emphasis may be organized differently from a project where schedule or budget have priority.

Although the form of organization may differ, there are certain characteristics common to all. An effective organization must be flexible, responsive, efficient, and clear:

❑ An effective project organization is **flexible** and responsive to change. Office design projects have a tendency to grow or contract. Schedules slip and budgets may be exceeded. Personnel may be reassigned and others take their place. A project organization must be able to adapt.

❏ An effective project organization is **responsive** to the needs of the project, the client, and the design firm. Small projects require small teams with a variety of tasks performed by each individual. Large projects need large teams with greater individual specialization. A high design project may be organized to allow greater latitude to the project designer. A fast-track project may emphasize the role of the project manager.

❏ An effective project organization recognizes the potential of its members and uses those talents as **efficiently** and **productively** as possible. Individual team members will have differing interests and abilities, and these often do not align perfectly with idealized job descriptions. Although an able team leader may lack an interest in paperwork and a talented designer may lack presentation skills, these conditions may not necessarily affect team effectiveness. A good organization adapts itself to people, not the other way around.

❏ An effective project organization has a **clarity** and **simplicity** of structure that is clearly understood by each team member. The authority and accountability of each team member should be well defined. Each team member should know his or her role and how that role fits into the overall structure. A great deal of time may be wasted and errors committed by team members who aren't doing the right job or who don't know what is expected.

There are many forms that a project organization may assume. Three examples might be called the matrix, the pyramid, and the wagon wheel.

Departmental Matrix Organization

The *departmental matrix* organization is common in large design firms and is most appropriate for large projects. The permanent project team under this type of structure consists of a project manager, sometimes called the account executive, and perhaps several assistants. It is the

	PROGRAM DEPT.	DESIGN DEPT.	DOCUMENT DEPT.	FIELD DEPT.
PROJECT A				
PROJECT B				
PROJECT C				

DEPARTMENTAL MATRIX STRUCTURE. Personnel are assigned to projects from their respective departments as needed.

responsibility of the project manager to maintain the liaison with the client and to shepherd the project through various specialized departments within the design firm, such as programming, design, documentation, and contract administration. In consultation with the project manager, the head of each specialty department assigns individuals to perform specific tasks for the project on an as-needed basis. When a task is complete, the individual reports back to the department head for reassignment. The department head is responsible for quality control for the particular specialty.

The advantage of the departmental matrix organization is high quality and efficient production owing to specialization. The disadvantages are lack of continuity and follow-up and diminished personnel challenge, motivation, and commitment. This type of organization is often viewed as an assembly line, lacking design innovation and with limited opportunities for growth. The departmental matrix organization is more common on large building design or engi-neering work than on office interiors projects.

Pyramidal Team Organization

A *pyramidal team* structure consists of a group of people organized in a hierarchical reporting arrangement. The team may be led by a project manager, a project designer, or both. In smaller firms these roles may be filled by the principals of the firm. In larger firms, team leaders may report to the principals or to project directors who are responsible for a number of teams. Team members are assigned for the duration of the project and perform all project tasks in all phases with help from outside specialists kept to a minimum.

The advantage of the pyramidal organization is continuity and personnel commitment and motivation. Decisions are followed through from phase to phase. The disadvantage may be some loss of efficiency. The pyramidal organization is particularly appropriate to projects requiring creativity, adaptability, and continuity.

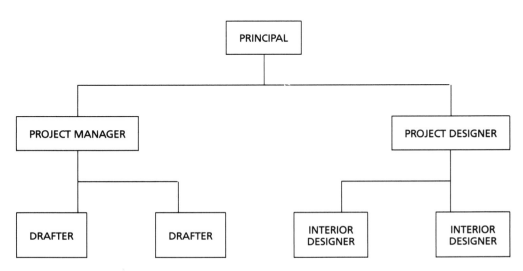

PYRAMIDAL TEAM STRUCTURE. *Personnel are assigned to the team for the duration of the project.*

Wagon Wheel Organization

A departmental matrix structure and a pyramidal team structure both depend on delegation, the ability to direct another person to perform a task as well as one would do it oneself. This is a rare skill. Those with this ability multiply their effectiveness many times over. Most people, however, would "rather do it themselves."

A project organization that minimizes delegation is the *wagon wheel*. In this model, one person, usually the project manager, stands at the hub and personally directs every aspect of the project. This is the simplest, most common, and, for many projects, most effective structure. It is the basic structure for the vast majority of design firms, where there are fewer than ten people and decision making is concentrated in the principal.

The wagon wheel becomes even more effective if mirrored by a strong facility manager in the client organization. The structure minimizes communication and thus reduces errors and misunderstandings. Decisions are made quickly and work produced efficiently. However, the structure is effective only on small projects with teams of fewer than five to seven members and requires the dedicated services of a highly capable individual whose talents might better be used on larger projects.

From the many possible team structures, most design firms tend to standardize on a few that have been found to be effective. An advantage of this standardization is that, over time, the roles of each position become well defined and well understood, and little time is wasted teaching team members new systems and procedures. Each team's success is easy to evaluate against other project teams. The danger is that the standardized teams may become stale and unresponsive to project needs. Individuals may come to feel they are being underutilized, forced into slots where they don't fit, and prevented from advancing. When the form becomes more important than the content, even the most efficient and successful firms can benefit from a reevaluation of their systems and procedures.

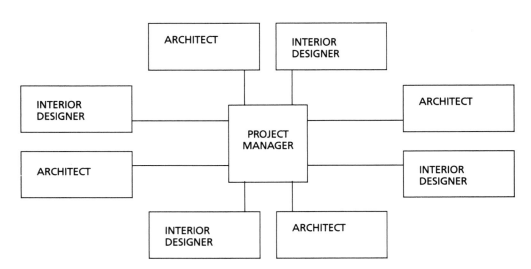

WAGON-WHEEL STRUCTURE. All team members report directly to the project manager.

Client Organization

The need for organization is not confined to the design team. Project organization is required on the part of the client as well. On the client's part, there are generally three major functional groups or constituencies that must be identified, organized, and satisfied.

Overall project direction and major project decisions including design and budget are the responsibility of the *senior management* of the client firm, often the chief executive officer. Sometimes this function is assumed by a group of senior executives who form a building committee or space committee.

The client's *facility management group* may be responsible for project implementation including administration, scheduling, budgeting, and day-to-day work with the consultants and contractors. In small organizations this function may be performed by the office manager or by another designated executive. In larger organizations this function may be the responsibility of the facility manager and his or her staff, which may include a purchasing agent, a telecommunications expert, a director of construction, and many others.

The third group, the *users*, consists of the personnel who will actually occupy the new offices. They have detailed knowledge of the working requirements for the new offices and provide the designer with program data. As plans are developed, the users review them for functional acceptability. On small projects, meetings with users may be scheduled by the facility manager. On larger projects a formal user organization may be appropriate to identify user representatives who will work with the design consultants.

Whenever possible, the design firm organization and the client organization should mirror each other with parallel authority levels in each organization. Design firm principals may echo the client's senior executives, the design firm's project manager may parallel the client's facility manager, and the space planner may correspond to the user representatives. In addition to developing effective working relationships, parallel structures provide a means of conflict resolution. They allow disagreements at one level to be referred to the next higher level in an organized and nonconfrontational manner.

PROJECT ROLES

Whatever the project organization selected, it should be clearly comprehended by each team member. Team members should understand their roles on the project, who they report to, and what is expected.

Project roles should be explicitly defined by the twin concepts of accountability and authority. Accountability is that for which the individual is answerable to his or her superior. Authority is the power to accomplish a task. They must be equivalent; one cannot exist without the other. A job captain accountable for the production of a set of documents must have the authority to command manpower sufficient to the task. A project manager accountable for meeting a schedule must have the authority to set priorities and deadlines.

It is often useful to formalize the authority and accountability of each team member with a written job description. Typical job descriptions for a principal, project manager, project designer, and job captain might be:

Principal: Establishes overall goals and objectives of the firm. Sets quality standards. Negotiates contract; and monitors project fees, budgets, and schedules. Maintains senior-level client contact. Assigns team members, monitors employee performance, and gives raises. Resolves conflicts at the highest level.

Project Manager: Oversees the day-to-day administration of the project. Meets the terms of the professional service contract. Organizes the team and provides leadership and motivation. Assigns tasks and coordinates work. Prepares budgets and schedules and is directly responsible for cost and fee control. Maintains working client contact. Assists in the negotiation of contracts for construction and furnishings.

Project Designer: Sets functional and aesthetic goals of the project. Develops and presents the project program, space plans, and design concept. Selects materials and furnishings. Coordinates budgets, schedules, and staff assignments with the project manager.

Job Captain (sometimes called Project Architect): Oversees the preparation of contract documents. Checks for code compliance. Coordinates with engineers. Coordinates budgets, schedules, and staff assignments with the project manager and project designer. Works with contractors and observes the progress of construction in the field. Reviews shop drawings and prepares punch lists.

These descriptions will vary from project to project and should be tailored to the interests and abilities of individuals. There may be other roles that should be identified and described. Depending on the needs of the project, client, and design firm, these descriptions may change, expand, contract, or be combined.

PROJECT COMMUNICATION

A characteristic of the design process is its complexity. It consists of thousands of tiny details of many different types requiring a wide variety of methods of communication and documentation. There are many different people to keep informed about project-related issues. The details range from the dimensions of an office to the color of a chair fabric to the sound rating of a ceiling tile to the schedule for carpet installation. To be effectively implemented, projects require good communication. The means of communication may include drawings, models, words, figures, graphs, and samples.

Good communication minimizes errors. The consequences of error in office design can be significant. A small mistake on the drafting board can loom very large on the job site. A dimension that is incorrect by a fraction of an inch may require demolition and reconstruction of a partition. A transposed figure in a furniture order may mean that red chairs are supplied instead of blue. A misunderstanding about a room location may result in a serious operational burden.

Too many such errors may lead to hostility, lawsuits, dismissal of the design firm, and a failed project. To avoid these problems precise documentation is required; documentation that is not only produced but checked, rechecked, reviewed, and approved. Communication is often made more difficult because of "language." Lawyers communicate primarily with words, and accountants use figures. The primary means of communication for architects and interior designers is drawings. Design professionals may find themselves, in essence, speaking a foreign language to a client who cannot read drawings. Conversely, the design professional can easily miss a verbal nuance of great importance to the client.

Establishing project forms and procedures during the project initiation period helps avoid such communication errors and misunderstandings. By formalizing procedures a system of checks and balances is put in place that makes communication faster and more accurate. It provides a framework or context within which communication takes place. Team members are then conditioned to know how to respond. Although letters, transmittals, memoranda, meeting minutes, and change orders are each forms of written communication, they differ in type of content, urgency, and priority, and each prompts a different type of response.

Many design firms have graphically coordinated standardized formats for project management and implementation. These may be printed forms or templates stored in word-processing software, where they may be easily accessed and revised. The project initiation period is an opportunity for both design firm and client to introduce each other to the forms and formats each intends to use on the project.

As a communication and record-keeping device, standard forms have many advantages. They avoid the necessity of "reinventing the wheel" each time a repetitive type of document is produced. They prompt the writer to prevent important elements of the communication from being forgotten. They condition the recipient to know how to respond.

There are also disadvantages. Forms have an insidious habit of taking over. Unless controlled, much time can be wasted filling out forms and documenting information of little practical use either to the project, the design firm, or the client. It should not be forgotten that standard forms are meant to simplify and speed the process. When they cease to perform this function they should be revised or discarded.

Standardized formats for architects and interior designers may include drafting sheets, meeting notes, address lists, telephone logs, accounting forms, contract forms, various change forms, materials schedules, shop drawing logs, and punch lists. Three of the most useful are transmittals, letters, and memoranda.

Transmittals

A *transmittal* is used when sending drawings or other documents between organizations. It is easier and faster than writing a letter. A standard transmittal contains the date, the recipient's name and address, a description of what is being sent, the purpose, the action to be taken by the recipient, the sender's name and address, and a list of others being copied with the same information.

Notes or comments on a transmittal should be brief. A transmittal itself should not be used to convey substantive information. A letter should be used instead. The most important element of the transmittal may be its distribution list. When sending the same material to several parties, one transmittal is used showing the prime recipient and listing the others to be copied. This not only saves time but lets each recipient know who else has received the same information.

It is often useful to establish standard distribution lists for various types of information. This can avoid complaints and misunderstanding later on from those who thought they should receive something but didn't, as well as from those who object to being overwhelmed by paperwork.

Letters

For all their usefulness, transmittals

TRANSMITTAL

Date: August 16, 19—

To: J. Walter Dudley
             TREDWAY FURNITURE CORPORATION
             Tredway Tower
             Millburgh, PA 01578

Via: Overnight Delivery

Project: Federal Broadcasting
             Records Department Remodeling

Job No.:   1491.00

Items: 4 prints   A4/4th Floor Furniture   8/8/—
             4 prints   A8/Custom Details   8/8/—
             4 prints   A9/Custom Details   8/8/—
             1 set   Preliminary Furniture Specs   8/5/—

             For your review and comment

             1 sample   Wood finish TR8—78

             Approved for use in the mock-up

Remarks: Note our suggested bullnose detail on the credenza return,
             drawing 6/A8. Is this feasible? What are the cost implications?
             Please call after you have had a chance to review these drawings.

From: Jed Leland

CC: Bunny Watson/Federal Broadcasting
             Richard Sumner/Federal Broadcasting

KANE & LELAND/185 West 74th St/New York NY 10023/212—555—1941

TRANSMITTAL. This form is used to transmit drawings, samples, and other material. Comments and remarks should be kept to a minimum.

should not be used for formal or important communication. For those purposes a *letter* is generally more appropriate. All of the elements listed above for transmittals are present in a letter but in a more narrative form.

By its format, a letter commands more immediate attention than other forms of written communication and should be used whenever the full attention of the reader is vital. Letters should be used whenever making a formal submission in accordance with the design contract, such as asking for approval at the completion of a contract phase. Letters should be used when communicating matters of time and money, when asking a question, raising an issue, or giving an opinion.

Memoranda

An informal form of letter is the *memorandum*. It combines some of the standard features of a transmittal but is used to convey substantive information. Because of its informality, some design firms restrict its use to in-house communication.

MEETINGS AND PRESENTATIONS

A *meeting* is a forum for communication, for discussion, and for the transfer of information. *Presentations* are meetings specifically intended for decision making and for the approval of ideas. Meetings and presentations are a necessary part of the development of a project. However, no drawings are actually produced in meetings, and in this sense they are nonproductive. For this reason meetings and presentations should be tightly controlled and efficiently run.

A regular schedule of project meetings allows participants to anticipate and prepare. If the purpose and format is initially established and followed on a regular basis, each person knows what to expect

and is mentally prepared to both contribute and receive information effectively. There is no wasted time spent on the learning curve, trying to figure out what the meeting is for, who is in charge, what is to be accomplished.

A list of regularly schedules meetings on a typical office design project may look something like this:

Client project meeting, held once a week for two hours, chaired by the project manager.

Design firm's in-house design meeting, held once a week for one hour, chaired by the project manager.

Meeting with the engineers and other consultants, held once a week during the design development and documentation phase, chaired by the job captain.

Design presentations to the client's senior management, held once a month or in accordance with the project schedule, chaired by the project designer.

Field job meetings, held once a week on the job site, chaired by the contractor's field superintendent.

Meetings have a tendency to both proliferate and to grow in size. They have an aura of importance and are often convened when telephone calls or memoranda would accomplish the same thing. They have a tendency to become status symbols; those who attend are perceived to have knowledge not possessed by those who are left out. Consequently there is pressure to include more and more people to avoid giving offense. These tendencies should be strongly resisted. If there is no important business that requires a large group of people to be gathered in one place, the meeting should not be held. Meetings should be attended only by those are required to make a contribution. Others who need information may receive it through the meeting notes.

Meetings are official project activities and, as such, have legal implications. Meeting notes may be important evidence in case of legal action. So that all parties can be assured that they have complete information, each regularly scheduled meeting of each type may be consecutively numbered beginning at the start of the project through to completion. This meeting number is shown in both the agenda and meeting minutes.

Meetings should be chaired and the chairperson clearly identified. The chairperson generally represents the organization with the most pressing need for the meeting. He or she may be the design firm's project manager, the client's facility manager, the contractor's account executive, or another designated person. Among the duties of the chairperson are preparing and distributing the agenda, determining who should attend the meeting and informing them of time and place, arranging for the meeting room and refreshments, and making sure that outside interruptions during the meeting are minimized.

The chairperson's primary function is to maintain order, keep the meeting moving, and see that the purpose of the meeting is accomplished. He or she should keep the discussion on track. The chairperson should be alert for signs of unhappiness or unspoken dissent. All should be given an opportunity to express their opinion but digressions should be not allowed. Discussion should be courteous and tempers should be kept under control (as the Godfather said: "It's only business"). When a subject is concluded and a decision made,

---

MEETING AGENDA

Date: April 12, 19—, 10:00 a.m.

Project: Federal Broadcasting

Location: Kane and Leland

Subject: Weekly Job Meeting #7

1. Review of Minutes

2. Block Plan Status

3. Program Revisions
   a. Accounting Department
   b. Legal Department

4. Consultant Selection
   a. Mechanical Engineer
   b. Electrical Engineer
   c. Food Service Consultant

5. Acoustical Criteria

6. Graphics Status

7. Schedule Update
   a. Long Lead Items
   b. Telecommunications

8. Budget Update
   a. Carpet Budget
   b. Audio-visual Additions

9. New Items

MEETING AGENDA. Every formal meeting should have a written agenda.

MEETING REPORT

Date: September 2, 19—

Project: Federal Broadcasting

Location: Jobsite

Present: B. Watson/Federal Broadcasting
             J. Leland/Kane and Leland
             C. C. Baxter/General Contractor

Subject: Weekly Job Meeting #28

Discussion	Action	By
1. Construction is on schedule. The partition layout has been reviewed.	Drywall construction to begin 9/5/—.	CCB
2. Raised floor shop drawings will be submitted on 9/25/—.	Review by 10/5/—.	K&L
3. Millwork bids have been received. Tredway is the apparent low bidder. Bids were below estimate.	Award by 9/7/—.	CCB
4. A revision to wall fabric W2 will be presented on 9/12/—.	Decision required by 9/25/—.	FB
5. Plumbing bids have been received.	Award by 9/8/—.	CCB

By: Jed Leland

CC: All Present
             C. Kane

This report will stand as the record of this meeting unless written corrections are received within seven days.

KANE & LELAND/185 West 74th St/New York NY 10023/212–555–1941

MEETING REPORT. A meeting report should be prepared within a day or two after each formal meeting.

the chairperson should quickly direct the discussion to the next agenda item.

Every meeting needs a written *agenda*, prepared by the chairperson. This is the primary vehicle for enforcing order. Agenda items may be listed in order of importance and may begin with a review of the previous meeting's minutes. If someone must leave early or if some people need be present for only a few agenda items, the agenda is adjusted accordingly.

Each agenda item is introduced by the chairperson, presented by its proponent, discussed by the participants, and concluded. The conclusion may be a decision, direction for further action or follow-up by an individual or organization, or agreement to postpone the item to a later date. The meeting should then move quickly to the next agenda item.

Meetings should have strict time limits enforced by the chairperson. This puts pressure on the participants to stick to the point and avoid rambling digressions. There are times when some people would rather sit and chat and put off doing more productive things. This is not the function of a meeting and wastes the time of those with more urgent tasks to attend to.

Meetings should seldom last beyond two hours, when even the most dedicated participants begin to tire. The best length for high productivity is between one and one-and-a-half hours.

Meetings and presentations should be minuted. Written minutes or meeting reports may be prepared by the chairperson or another individual at the chairperson's direction. The function of meeting reports is to record the action taken on each agenda item. For this reason, the format of meeting reports may consist of columns; one for identification and discussion of the item and one to record the decision or action to be taken. For ease of

reference each item should be numbered. The writing should be clear and concise; outline form is generally acceptable. In addition to substantive matters, meeting notes should record the name and number of the project, the location, date, and time of the meeting, the subject of the meeting, a list of participants, the name, address, and telephone and facsimile number of the author, the date the notes were prepared, and a distribution list.

Meeting minutes should be prepared as soon as possible after conclusion of the meeting, definitely before the next meeting. Copies are sent to each participant and other interested or affected parties. Each is invited to review and make corrections as necessary. Meeting minutes can be crucial information. If disagreements, misunderstandings, or legal action occur later on, meeting reports may be primary source documents for resolution. To encourage response and for protection against future problems, a disclaimer is often printed at the bottom of meeting notes such as: "This report will stand as the record of this meeting unless written corrections are received within seven days."

A review of notes from the preceding meeting is often the first item on an agenda. This may be another opportunity for corrections to be recorded and for the chairperson to review the results of action items.

ACCOUNTING PROCEDURES

Effective project management requires accurate accounting if the project is to be profitable for the design firm. The project manager is generally accountable to the design firm's principals for fee control and client invoicing. The firm's accountant or accounting department assists the project manager in fulfilling this obligation. To make this process work, the pro-

---

PROJECT INITIATION REPORT

Date: September 2, 19—

Project: Federal Broadcasting/Records Department Remodeling

Job No.:   1491.00

Manager: Jed Leland

Location: Federal Broadcasting Building/Floor 4
10543 Euclid Boulevard
Cleveland, Ohio 45060

Client: Ms. Bunny Watson/Director of Research
Research and Records Department

FEDERAL BROADCASTING CORPORATION
10543 Euclid Boulevard
Cleveland, Ohio 45060

Telephone: 216–555–1957

Facsimile: 216–555–1959

Contract: Letter contract dated 5/3/—, accepted 5/8/—

Fees: Hourly at standard flat rates to a maximum of:

Programming	$ 3,600
Design	5,400
Documents	9,400
Observation	6,600
Contingency	2,500
Total Fee Maximum	27,500

Consultants: Not Applicable, to be retained by client

Reimbursables: At cost plus 10%

Comments:

By: Jed Leland

PROJECT INITIATION REPORT. The project initiation report should record all pertinent financial data on a project for use by the accountant or the accounting department for billing and fee control. It should be conscientiously updated as required.

ject manager provides the accountant with project and contract information and the project team submits periodic time sheets. In return the accountant prepares client invoices and fee expenditure information for the project manager.

A project manager should expect to spend a significant amount of time each month in the preparation of accurate information and the review of accounting reports. This is a prime example of the theory of "garbage in, garbage out." If the information provided by the project manager and team is incorrect or incomplete, the fee reports will be worthless or, even worse, misleading about the fee status of the project.

There are many methods and systems available to provide project financial information. There are computer services dedicated to the design professions, accounting firms willing to provide systems and advice, and computer software packages available on the market. Generally these methods and systems are an integral part of the design firm's overall accounting system. Although they vary widely in detail and complexity, there are concepts common to all of them.

Project Initiation Report

When a project comes into a design firm and a contract is written, the details of the financial arrangements need to be entered into the firm's accounting system. This may be done by a *project initiation report*, which is completed by the project manager. The exact content of this form will be dictated by the system being used, but generally the report should contain the name and job number of the project, the client's name and address, projected fees (and hours) broken down by phase or subproject, the type of fee arrangement, hourly rates applicable to the project, and contract provisions regarding consultants and reimbursable costs.

This document is often submitted before a design contract is executed and may not indicate the final fee agreement. As time goes on there may be revisions to fee arrangements. The project manager needs to keep the accountant informed by updating the project initiation report.

Time Sheet

The basic document for recording team activity is the *time sheet*, which is filled out by each team member. This contains the employee's name and number, the project name, number, phase, and task, and the dates and hours worked.

Time sheets are generally submitted semi-monthly although some firms require weekly or even daily time sheets. Some firms require project managers to review and approve time sheets before submittal to the accountant. This is primarily to check the accuracy of the project number, phase, and task designations and may prevent tedious accounting changes later on.

Expense Reports

Expense reports are necessary if the design firm is to be compensated for reimbursable expenses. These should be submitted by team members in a timely fashion; many clients object to paying for expenses that are many months old or are for project phases that have been completed and closed out.

Project Progress Report

To complete the reports prepared by the project team and submitted to the firm's accountant, project managers may prepare a periodic *project progress report*. Through examination of drawings and knowledge of work performed, the project manager estimates the percentage complete of each phase or task on the project.

Fee Status Reports

By using the project initiation report, time cards, and project progress reports, the accounting system can generate project *fee status reports*. These can be formatted in a variety of ways to maximize their usefulness to the project manager. The information might include fees (and hours) spent to date by person, project, and phase; fees (and hours) spent compared to projected fees (and hours) and the percentage difference between the two; fees (and hours) spent compared to reported progress and the percentage difference between the two; fees spent compared to fees billed to date; and comparisons of actual consultants' fees and reimbursable expenses against projections.

FEE STATUS REPORT

Date: August 15, 19—

Project: Federal Broadcasting/Records Department Remodeling

For work through 7/31/—

Job No.	Phase	Max	%	Reported Spent	Actual Spent	Var.
	BASIC SERVICES					
1491.00	Program	3,960	100	3,960	3,400	560
	Design	5,940	100	5,940	6,300	(360)
	Document	10,340	65	6,721	6,200	521
	Observe	7,260	0	0	0	0
	Subtotal	27,500	60	16,621	15,900	721
	ADDITIONAL SERVICES					
1491.01	Revision A	4,400	100	4,400	4,100	300
1491.02	Revision B	2,300	40	920	1,200	(280)
1491.03	Artwork	1,200	25	300	200	100
	Subtotal	7,900	71	5,620	5,500	120
	Total	35,400	63	22,241	21,400	841

FEE STATUS REPORT. In this example of a fee status report, the project manager reports the percentage complete of each phase, each month, based on his or her analysis of project progress. The accountant calculates the fees that should have been spent based on this percentage and compares it with the fees that actually were spent based on time cards. The variance is a guide to the financial health of the project.

Two different fundamental approaches may be used in developing fee status reports: cost-based or billing-rate-based. A *cost-based* status report is set up to reflect a project's costs for salaries and overhead with profit shown as a resultant; it shows the difference between cost and what was billed to the client. The project manager's responsibility is then to maximize profit consistent with the level of service promised in the contract.

In contrast, a *billing-rate-based* status report shows team members' billing rates, which include salaries, overhead, and a factor for profit. Since profit is built in, each hour spent times its billing rate equals the amount expected to be billed. The project manager's responsibility is to match hours spent to projected fees.

The cost-based reporting system is most appropriate for analyzing overall office performance. The billing-rate-based approach, however, is probably better for project management on individual projects.

Invoices

The accounting department also produces *invoices* for services and reimbursable expenses. The format for this document will depend on the billing method specified in the contract. An invoice for services provided on an hourly basis will show the names of those who have worked on the project, the hours spent, their billing rates, and the total fees being billed by phase.

For projects billed on a percentage basis, the invoice will show the total contracted fee by phase multiplied by the percent complete to show the total earned fee to date. Previous billings are deducted to arrive at the invoice amount.

Draft invoices are generally reviewed for accuracy by the project manager, and, as a final check, some firms require that the project manager sign the invoice before it is sent to the client. Some project managers like to send a personal letter with the invoice giving a narrative explanation of the invoice or a report on progress during the previous month. They feel that this personalization of the process helps client relations and may speed payment.

Design firms sometimes find that payment for design fees is delayed for purely technical reasons; the invoice, for example, may have been lost in a chain of approvals, or some detail might be incompatible with the client's own accounting system. This is common when the client is a very large or bureaucratic organization. To avoid these problems, it is often helpful for the design firm accountant to meet with his or her opposite number in the client organization to gain an understanding of the payment and approval process and to lay the groundwork for communication if the need arises.

Sometimes invoices are unpaid for other reasons. An unpaid invoice might indicate dissatisfaction with the service provided or disagreement about the amount charged. This requires immediate attention by the project manager or the principal of the firm. Sometimes invoices are unpaid because of client financial problems or a client perception that payment to architects and interior designers is a low priority. In these cases, design firms should be prepared to stop work, per the professional service contract, until the issue is resolved.

CHAPTER FOUR

SITE SELECTION

Before design and construction can begin, a site must be selected. For an office interiors project, this site will be an existing or proposed office building. There are a variety of options available. A company may choose to rent space from a new building constructed by a developer or corporate owner. It may decide to buy land and construct its own building or make a build-to-suit arrangement with a developer. It may decide to stay where it is and expand or remodel. Or the company may purchase or lease an older building and renovate to suit its needs.

Selecting the right location is one of the most important decisions to be made in the development of new office space, and adequate time should be allowed. Analyzing options and negotiating specific lease terms can be a lengthy process. It is not unusual for a large company to spend several years and evaluate ten or fifteen different locations before making a selection. A company that waits until its existing lease is about to expire may find its choices severely limited.

In choosing a building for lease, a company may find a number of properties that are appealing. It is unlikely, however, that one building will be the best in all respects. One may have an ideal location, another will offer an attractive rent, and a third may provide desirable expansion options. The advantages and disadvantages of each building should be systematically analyzed and priorities set.

Site selection is a fluid process. As soon as one set of options is systematically arranged, new problems and opportunities may pop up. Nevertheless, the development of an organized *site selection analysis* is usually worth the effort. As a listing and evaluation of facts and priorities, this analysis should be of great help during lease negotiations and final selection.

One option available to most companies is to stay put—to renegotiate an existing lease, or to expand or remodel its current premises. An advantage of including existing facilities in the site selection analysis is that they are a known quantity, a benchmark against which other properties may be compared. A major disadvantage is that construction in existing, occupied space may cause great inconvenience. Swing space may have to be found for the temporary relocation of personnel, or the construction may have to be phased, which will probably increase the cost.

A site selection analysis will vary in form and content depending on the situation. If the major decision is whether to buy, to build, or to lease, the analysis will concentrate on a detailed economic analysis of the options. If the issue to be decided is the location from among a number of suburban communities, the analysis may emphasize demographics and tax considerations. If the choice is among similar urban high-rise office buildings, rental rates, building and landlord quality, and program compatibility may be most important.

CONSULTANTS

Much of the work involved in site selection analysis can be done in-house, particularly if the company has an active real estate or facility management department. Usually, however, outside experts are consulted. A real estate broker may be the best source for a comparison of location and lease rates, terms and conditions, as well as assistance in lease negotiation. A broker who represents a property under consideration will provide information about that property. For an evaluation and comparison of various competing buildings, a trusted real estate agent who does not directly represent any of the buildings under consideration may be in a position to objectively advise and represent the tenant. Compensation for the real estate broker is typically a commission paid by the building owner when a lease is consummated.

Two consultants that should always be retained are an experienced real estate attorney, regarding the terms and conditions of the lease, and an accountant, who will examine financial and tax implications.

For an evaluation of building quality, construction alternatives, and architectural fit with the space program, an architect or interior designer may be involved. These services are usually not included in the basic fee for interior planning and design but are paid for as an additional service on an hourly or other basis.

Depending on the complexity of the project, other consultants that may contribute to site analysis include mechanical, electrical, and structural engineers and general contractors, construction managers, or cost estimators. A consultant in building operations may be useful to check operating expenses.

PRELIMINARY PROGRAMMING

Before the analysis of options can begin, the approximate floor area required by the new office space must be determined, as well as an estimate of expansion option space that may be required for future growth needs. One way of determining this is from the detailed space program. Unfortunately, few project schedules allow the luxury of an orderly sequence of programming, followed by site selection and then design. On the other hand, even the most detailed program is only accurate to within about 10 percent, and this same level of accuracy can be achieved in a simpler way.

Most organizations have long-range staff projections, annual business plans, or other documents that attempt to project staff needs. Total required occupiable, or *carpetable*, area can be quickly calculated by estimating the area required per person through an examination of existing space or from industry standards. This area, multiplied by the expected population, plus allowances for special areas such as cafeterias or computer rooms should give a *preliminary program* that is accurate enough for site analysis and lease negotiation.

Option space requirements are generally based on long-range growth projections. Accuracy decreases as time spans increase. A primary objective in the negotiation for option space is to preserve as much flexibility as possible with regard to size, location, and timing.

LOCATION

Selecting the right geographic location for the new office is usually the easiest decision to be made, particularly for smaller projects. The choice between urban and suburban, or high-rent district versus low-rent is usually obvious. Very large projects, however, may require detailed demographic, cost, and tax studies.

Every city has what the real estate community considers to be the "100 percent corner," the best location in town. This designation is assigned in part because this location has the easiest access for the most people. It is also because this location has the most prestige, the best image. This image influences public perception, and as a result the companies who occupy this spot are often automatically considered the best in their field. These locations command premium rents.

If an organization has the need for high customer contact, accessibility and visibility become of prime importance. A central business district location may be crucial to a professional service firm whose customers are other downtown businesses.

By contrast, some companies like to maintain a low profile or are more cost conscious. Some may deal with customers only by telephone, mail, or an outside sales staff. These organizations may prefer a lower-rent location, outside of the central business district.

Neighborhoods of similar businesses seem to develop naturally in some cities. Some types of offices tend to congregate around specialized facilities. Doctors cluster around hospitals and shipping firms like to be near harbors or airports. There are garment districts, theater districts, and artists' colonies. Law firms congregate around courthouses. Universities are magnets for office users engaged in research activities.

Some locations have become so closely identified with certain industries as to become symbols of the businesses located there. Wall Street has become synonymous with the stock market and Hollywood means movies. So many computer firms have located near Palo Alto, California, drawn in part by the proximity of Stanford University, that the area has became known as the Silicon Valley.

Historic renovations have their own special attractions. Besides inherent charm, they exude an aura of social and environmental consciousness that can enhance a company's image.

Good highway systems make suburban locations practical for large office-space users. This may be the operations center in a developer's office park or the luxury of a corporate headquarters hidden away in the forest.

Access to the site by employees may be either by public transportation or by private car. Central business district locations generally provide convenient bus, subway, or commuter rail access. For suburban offices, good access for automobiles with adequate parking is a necessity.

Suburban office buildings are often selected because of proximity to employees' homes. In the development of large operations centers, banks and insurance companies often undertake elaborate demographic studies to assist in selecting the location that will be most convenient and attractive to the largest number of existing and prospective employees.

Location amenities, such as the availability of food service, may affect building selection. Central business district locations usually offer employees a variety of places to eat ranging from fast food take-out to high-priced restaurants. Suburban locations generally offer much less choice. Where outside food service is limited, some landlords and tenants provide on-premises cafeterias. Owner occupants may find that they must subsidize food service for employees.

Other amenities include day-care and exercise facilities. Some buildings have conference centers with teleconferencing capability and meeting rooms that may be rented by the hour or by the day.

Like other major business decisions, many real estate deals hinge on tax considerations. Companies may be driven from urban locations into the suburbs to take advantage of lower taxes. To combat this trend and to attract new businesses, many cities are offering tax incentives that are hard to resist. In a similar vein, utility companies offer incentives in the form of construction and installation allowances and favorable rates to entice large consumers of utility services.

More often than many people would like to admit, locations for office facilities, particularly corporate headquarters, are picked because of the amenities and advantages they offer for corporate executives. Many Sun Belt locations are chosen this way. After all the quantitative analysis is completed, many office locations are selected simply because of the highly subjective preference of the boss.

RENT

Cost is important when selecting office space, and over time the biggest component of occupancy cost is rent.

Rent is generally quoted in dollars per square foot of *rentable area* per year. This is complicated by the fact that the definition of rentable area for an office building is the prerogative of the landlord, and landlords calculate rentable area in different ways. Sometimes rentable area equals *occupiable area*, which is the floor space available for the tenant's personnel and furnishings. This is the usual method of calculation for retail space. For office space, however, rentable area is typically increased by an allowance for core spaces and/or the addition of a *load factor*. The calculation method may be based on local custom, what landlords believe is fair, or, sometimes, what they believe the market will bear. The consequences can be significant. In rare instances, particularly in New York City, rentable area can be as much as 30 percent higher than occupiable area.

The rentable area concept is primarily a marketing strategy. The greater the rentable area, the lower the rate per rentable square foot. Although commonly accepted, the concept of rentable area adds a level of confusion to an already complex process. Nevertheless, it has a logical justification. The gross area of an office building is much higher than its occupiable office area. Furthermore, it is the nonoccupiable area that contains the most expensive systems of the building, such as the elevators, air conditioning plant, and ground floor lobby. Landlords rationalize that costs for these areas should be directly passed through to tenants. They do so by including a pro-rata share of the square footage of these common areas in the area calculation, by adding a percentage load factor, or both.

There is no legally enforceable definition of rentable area. There are, however, recognized national standard methods for computing rentable area such as those of the American Institute of Architects (AIA) and the Building Owners and

Managers Association (BOMA). Many local real estate boards promote these or other standard calculation methods within their regions. The General Services Administration (GSA) compels landlords to comply with its own method of measuring space when it leases office space for federal government use. Few private tenants, however, have the clout of the GSA, and most must accept the landlord's calculation method. Since buildings in the same neighborhood may use different methods of calculating rentable area, tenants should recalculate the rent for each property under consideration on an occupiable square foot basis to make an "apples-to-apples" comparison.

Typically a rentable area calculation for a full-floor tenant begins with the occupiable area that the GSA defines as "that portion of the gross area which is available for use by the occupant's personnel or furnishings." To this may be added the area of toilet rooms, elevator lobbies, electrical, telephone, and janitor's closets and other core rooms that serve only that particular floor. Not generally included are shafts for mechanical ductwork, elevators, and stairs. The result will be approximately what BOMA defines as rentable area. Many landlords will use this as the definition applicable to their buildings. Others may modify the definition in some way or may dispense with the calculation altogether, simply adding a percentage load factor to the occupiable area.

Smaller tenants on multiple tenant floors are treated in a similar way except that their area will include a pro-rata share of core rooms and the shared public corridor on the floor.

Area measurement is complicated. Apparently small differences in definition can have significant impact. For example, BOMA measures space to the inside wall surface of the exterior wall while GSA measures to the face of the convector unit (if it occupies at least 50 percent of the length of the exterior wall). These apparently minor variations in definition can affect rentable area by hundreds of square feet and rent by thousands of dollars per floor. Further subtleties in area measurement may involve the treatment of furred spaces and vestibules and whether the face of a partition or its centerline is used for measurement.

Because landlords control the measurement of space in their buildings, neither prospective tenants nor their design consultants should attempt their own calculations. Tenants who base decisions on their own guesses of the measurement rules can be cruelly surprised. A landlord-calculated rentable area should be a prerequisite for serious lease negotiations. Area calculations required of design firms should be limited to measurements of occupiable area using base building construction drawings or the verification of rentable area using the landlord's exact definition. If an exact building area is required, tenants might consider using a registered surveyor who will certify the results.

In theory, when market conditions favor tenants over landlords, everything in a lease for office space is negotiable. In practice, once the method for calculating rentable area is determined for a particular building, the formula generally will not be changed, landlords preferring to vary the rental rate instead. Other commonly negotiated concessions include free rent for a number of months, the assumption of lease payments in the vacated location, contributions toward construction costs above those provided in the workletter, and contributions toward moving expenses.

Rentable area calculations are not only used in lease situations. Managers of owner-occupied buildings often use rentable area calculations as a method of pro-rating occupancy costs between corporate departments or cost centers.

WORKLETTER CONSTRUCTION

Many leases for office space contain an attachment known as the *tenant workletter*. The workletter defines the quality and quantity of basic construction of the tenant's office space to be provided by the landlord. It generally includes minimum reasonable construction needed to allow for useful occupancy of the space. Thus tenants can theoretically move in with no out-of-pocket construction expense. Items typically include:

A basic heating, ventilating, and air conditioning (HVAC) system

An acoustical tile ceiling with fluorescent light fixtures and fire protection sprinklers

Electrical and telephone outlets

Full-height, painted partitions with base

Finished doors, frames, and standard hardware

Window coverings

Carpet or other floor covering

Quantities of each item are usually provided based on rentable square footage. Substitutions may be allowed provided the substituted item is of equal or better quality than the standard and the tenant pays for any additional cost. An exception is window coverings, where substitutions are usually not allowed in order to preserve the uniform exterior appearance of the building.

Construction of workletter items may be accomplished in a variety of ways. The landlord may provide workletter construction through its own general contractor or may offer to provide a dollar allowance against building standard construction provided by the tenant's general contractor. To maintain quality control, the landlord may limit the general contractors and subcontractors allowed to work in the building to those on a preapproved list. For their part, tenants may also wish to reserve the right to approve the contractors and subcontractors building their interior improvements.

Landlords like to include basic construction in workletters for reasons besides its value as a lease inducement. It allows them to control the quality of construction in their buildings. If they use their own general contractor, they can control the scheduling of construction and construction procedures. Finally, by buying items such as doors, hardware, light fixtures, and gypsum wallboard in quantity, money may be saved. Workletters in different buildings will vary in quality and cost. With the assistance of the design firm, engineering firm, construction manager, cost consultant, and/or general contractor, the value of a given workletter can be estimated. A translation into cost per occupiable square foot will allow a comparison between buildings.

Usually above-standard or decorative construction along with furnishings and equipment, design fees, moving costs, and various other expenses can be assumed to be equal regardless of which building is selected. They can therefore be ignored if the site selection analysis is to be used strictly as a comparison of options. If the analysis must also present a full picture of all costs connected with the project, these costs obviously must be estimated and included.

OTHER LEASE CONSIDERATIONS

Leasehold improvements, even above-standard construction paid for by the tenant, become the property of the landlord. These improvements generally must remain in place when a tenant moves out. Some leases require that if leasehold improvements such as cabinetwork are removed, the partitions that remain must be patched and repaired.

If heavy equipment or file rooms are to be installed by the tenant or if floor penetrations are required for tenant interior stairs or vertical conveyors, a structural feasibility and cost analysis may be advisable before a lease is signed.

Most leases require that tenant's construction drawings and specifications be submitted to the landlord at various stated times to be checked for conformance with building standards. Landlords often charge a fee for checking these documents, as well as for other administrative services in connection with construction.

Office leases contain dates for rent commencement that coincide with scheduled occupancy. Since landlords obviously want rent payments to begin as soon as possible, they may propose dates that represent greatly accelerated design and construction schedules. Dates may be based on estimated schedules for workletter construction only and may not take into account the time required for tenants' above-standard construction and new furniture delivery.

Building rules and regulations can affect construction and may have a significant cost impact for a tenant. For example, there may be a charge for the use of freight elevators, trash removal, or guard service. There may be limitations on the times and availability of elevators

and loading docks. Noisy work may have to be confined to overtime hours to avoid disturbing other tenants.

In older buildings, tenants are usually responsible for demolishing existing construction before new construction can begin. Costs for this work are usually reasonable unless asbestos is discovered. If asbestos is found it may have to be removed, encapsulated, or left undisturbed, depending on Environmental Protection Agency (EPA) or local regulations. This can be expensive. An investigation for the presence of asbestos by a qualified consultant or contractor should always be part of the analysis of older buildings before a lease is negotiated.

Building codes in most cities require that new office buildings be provided with automatic fire protection sprinkler systems. Some codes require that when older buildings not so equipped are remodeled, sprinklers must be added or other provisions for controlling the spread of fire must be installed. One method is compartmentation, the subdividing of the floor into small areas separated by fire-rated construction. The addition of this fire protection can be expensive and may reduce layout flexibility.

In addition to asbestos treatment and fire protection requirements, there may be other expensive construction required to bring the premises into compliance with current regulations, such as additional stairways or facilities for the disabled.

Options for additional space in the future may be a necessity for some organizations. Options typically will be for designated contiguous blocks of space that will become available at specific future times, such as in three, five, or ten years.

To develop a full picture of the cost of new office space, estimates may be developed for these additional lease costs. As with construction costs, a conversion into cost per occupiable square foot will allow different buildings to be most accurately compared.

BUILDING QUALITY

Buildings vary widely in quality. This is a function of the care with which they are designed and the money invested in construction and maintenance. A building may have a *signature* quality, a design by a well-known architect destined to become the standard of excellence and a landmark within the community. For a qualitative assessment of building and construction quality, tenants may seek the advice of their design and engineering consultants. Factors to be considered are:

Reputation of the developer, architect, engineers, and contractors

Design of landscaping, plazas, paving, and exterior lighting

Exterior and interior signage

Exterior materials and quality of construction detailing

Views from office floors

Provision of open or enclosed parking, ease of access from the street, the ratio of the number of parking spaces to the occupiable area of the building, and the number and location of spaces reserved exclusively for each tenant's use

Ground-floor lobby size, finishes, design, and provision for security and visitor information

Service access, loading dock design, size and number of truck docks, the number and size of freight elevators, and provision of service lobbies on office floors

Quantity, design, speed, and capacity of passenger elevators

Floor loading capacity and ease of structural reinforcing for file rooms or other areas

Design criteria, quality, and capacity of the heating, ventilating, and air conditioning (HVAC) system, the number and size of zones on office floors, the capacity to provide for computer room, food service, and conference room needs, and provision for after hours, weekend, or twenty-four-hour service

Size of electrical service, provision of separate circuits for computers or other equipment, provision for signal cabling, and provision of such "intelligent" building systems as a central telecommunications system

Number of fixtures and quality of finishes in public toilet rooms and wet columns or other provisions for remote plumbing for coffee stations or executive washrooms

Finishes, lighting, and graphics in public areas of multiple tenant floors and ease of circulation and width of public corridors

Life safety systems and provision for the disabled

Storage areas available to tenants

Quality of building maintenance

For buildings not yet constructed, a commitment to become a major tenant may provide the opportunity to participate in or alter the base building design. Structural, electrical, and HVAC capacity may be tailored to the tenant's needs. Elevatoring may be adjusted, finishes upgraded, and the design and layout of the core may be changed. A major tenant may be able to name the building, a benefit that may have significant public relations value.

HYPOTHETICAL SPACE PLANNING

Within certain broad ranges, most well-designed, modern buildings can satisfy the needs of most organizations. This is no accident. Developers know their markets and build accordingly. Professional service firms, corporate headquarters, and banking operations centers each have floor plan requirements that are met by different basic building footprints. The discovery of the suitability of a particular footprint to meet a particular tenant's space program is the function of the *hypothetical space plan*.

A hypothetical space plan is a diagrammatic floor layout prepared by an architect or interior designer showing relationships of generic or idealized space types such as private offices, open workstations, and corridors. It is not intended to be a detailed design solution for a specific program. Its aim is to test in broad terms whether there is a reasonable fit between the building and a tenant's needs. Hypothetical space plans can also be used to validate preliminary estimates of overall square footage requirements and as a rough guide to a building's efficiency in terms of space use.

There is a temptation to try to be too definitive in this process, to use a program with too much detail and produce space plans with too much "design." This can result in a study of interior design concepts rather than an analysis of the qualities and potential of the building.

If the detailed space program for the project has been completed, its summary results can be used as a basis for the hypothetical space plans. If not, a preliminary program may be quickly developed. This should be quite schematic. It should include the approximate number of people in each type of open workstation and private office, and an approximation of the area required for support facilities, such as conference rooms and file areas, and special facilities, such as computer rooms and cafeterias. For large projects, preliminary programs for selected typical departments or areas may be all that is necessary.

Using the preliminary program the architect or interior designer can prepare any number of hypothetical space plans for each building or floor footprint under consideration. These diagrams might be single line drawings showing circulation paths with simple rectangles indicating offices and open workstations. When doing diagrams for alternative buildings, every effort should be made to keep the program constant so that the limitations and opportunities of each property are highlighted.

One result of the hypothetical space plans may be a determination of the optimum overall floor size and the most appropriate distance from the building core to windows. Small floors with shallow core-to-window dimensions favor organizations with a need for many private offices such as law firms; large floors with deep core-to-window dimensions are more appropriate for large bank or insurance company operations centers using open-office workstations.

Another result is an analysis of the effect of window mullion spacing on the size of perimeter offices. A four-foot window mullion spacing, for example, will allow office widths of eight, twelve, sixteen, and twenty feet. A five-foot spacing encourages widths of ten, fifteen, and twenty feet. The cumulative effect of this spacing might affect overall floor efficiency. Irregular window placement at the perimeter brings different problems and opportunities that may be revealed in the layouts.

The hypothetical space plan may reveal the effect of structural column spacing on the floor layout. In open office spaces, the column spacing may establish the logical rhythm for the placement of workstations. Interior column spacing may limit the ability to accommodate an auditorium or large meeting rooms or may inhibit sight lines in stock trading rooms. At the perimeter, column spacing should be checked for compatibility with the arrangement of private offices.

Modular, rectangular floor footprints with center cores will generally prove to be most efficient in an idealized sense. They may be the most flexible, as they are relatively easy to change, expand, and sublease if necessary. On the other hand, this does not mean that they will be the best for the final office design. Buildings with irregular shapes and off-center cores often possess creative possibilities that, in the hands of an imaginative architect or interior designer, can result in efficient as well as attractive offices. Hypothetical space plans can only scratch the surface of these design possibilities. Care should be taken not to reject a building because its planning potential is not immediately obvious.

CHAPTER FIVE

PROGRAMMING

Programming is the process of gathering and analyzing information about an organization for use in the planning and design of office space. The end result of this process is the *space program*. This document contains qualitative information concerning organizational goals, culture, operations, and adjacencies, and quantitative data about planning unit and workplace growth, size, and configuration.

Traditionally, the program for an architectural project was developed in-house by the owner and given to the architect at the time he or she was hired. Because of increasing complexity, most projects today, and particularly office planning projects, require programs developed by specialists, either design firms or firms dedicated exclusively to providing programming services.

A secondary, but very important, purpose of the programming process is the establishment by the architect or interior designer of an effective working relationship and credibility with the client. In any organization there is an atmosphere, a spirit, a personality, that cannot be captured in a formal report but that must be absorbed by the design firm in order to effectively design the project. These factors argue strongly for programming to be performed by the design firm that will continue with the project through completion. On the other hand, a specialized programming firm may be able to bring

to the project an objectivity untinged by design bias and an efficiency based on specialization.

Space programming should not be confused with computer programming, although computers are indispensable for programming all but the smallest projects. There are a variety of computer software programs for space programming, some of which are tied to CADD software for project design and documentation. These are useful for very large or complex projects. For most projects, however, spreadsheet or data base manager software is sufficient and formats are easy to develop. Many space programmers believe these to be preferable since the formats and reports may be easily customized to the needs of the particular client organization.

A space program deals with planning, design, construction, and furnishings with which architects and interior designers are presumed to be expert, and not with organizational or operational issues that are more properly handled by management consultants, attorneys, and accountants. An architect or interior designer should be expected to design a file room or select a filing cabinet but not to reorganize a filing system. In reality, the experienced design professional may be able to contribute valuable suggestions regarding operational matters, but this should be accepted for what it is; advice that is above and beyond the scope of the architect's or interior designer's work and professional expertise.

Preconceptions about design solutions should be avoided during programming. They may introduce bias into the information gathering process. An architect or interior designer should have a clean slate when design begins to be able to explore the widest range of options. He or she needs objective fact and opinion, not information clouded by an unconscious effort to justify a design preference.

A space program is a working document that should be expected to change frequently. If periodically updated as a facility management tool, a space program can track the physical evolution of an organization to provide a valuable resource for future planning. Change, however, can be disruptive to the design and construction process. Typically a space program is frozen early in the schematic design phase of a project. Revisions can, and usually will, happen after that point but, unless limited and carefully controlled, they may adversely affect the overall schedule or budget.

There is often a tendency in space programming to try to gather too much information. For example, it may appear to be important for equipment placement to know which individuals are left-handed and which right-handed. However, given the rate at which employees move around within a typical organization, such detail is probably irrelevant to the design of a standard workstation. If "handedness" is an issue, a better solution is to configure workstations with the flexibility to accommodate either situation.

Similarly, while it may be interesting to know how many minutes each day each person spends talking on the telephone, writing memos, or reading correspondence, it is questionable whether this information will affect the selection of a new desk or chair. Programming is an expensive and time-consuming process, and the information sought should bear directly on the needs of the project.

Programming includes an information-gathering phase and an analysis phase. The information required is both quantitative and qualitative. Quantitative, statistical information is usually best obtained from formal, written surveys. Qualitative information is primarily gathered informally during interviews. Before either of these procedures begins, however, a thorough review should be conducted of existing conditions and existing information that may affect the project.

REVIEW OF EXISTING CONDITIONS

The first source of programming information is observation of the existing offices of the organization. This usually takes the form of a guided *tour* with copious note taking. The purpose of the tour is to gain a feel for the organization and how it operates. The tour may be repeated many times. Some programmers believe it is desirable to be able to know each person by name; to know who has the Van Gogh print and who has the Boston fern. They feel this helps to personalize the process and gain credibility.

A second source of information is a review of written and graphic *documents* that relate to the environmental needs of the organization. These include plans of existing office space, organization charts, staff lists, previous program and design studies, furniture inventories, purchase orders, and statements of corporate goals and objectives.

There is an element of serendipity in this search; one never knows just how valuable a piece of paper will be until it is looked at. Many companies, for example, take pride in elaborate organization charts that, on analysis, prove virtually worthless for space layout purposes, while sets of yellowing plans rolled up in a closet turn out to be invaluable for evaluating operational relationships.

STATISTICAL SURVEYS

Except on small projects, quantitative statistical data is best obtained through the use of formal written *surveys*. Information obtained in this way includes the number and type of each workplace in each unit, both existing and projected for several future dates. Survey forms generally also ask for narrative descriptions of function and adjacencies in anticipation of qualitative interviews. Although most design firms have preferred formats, survey forms are usually customized to meet the needs of each project.

Preparation for the survey includes designation of the units to be surveyed, determination of preliminary space standards, selection of planning dates, design of the actual survey form, and identification and orientation of the individuals who will complete the forms.

Planning Unit Designation

Every company has an organizational structure. This usually consists of a breakdown into divisions or departments that are related in some sort of hierarchy and formalized in an organization chart. This structure can provide the basic framework for a space program. The lowest level, say the department level, is the level at which data is collected and analyzed. It is the level used for adjacency studies, block planning, and space planning and may be used in the budgeting and scheduling of the project. However, since organizational structures are typically built around functional rather than spatial relationships, modifications to department designations are often required to make them useful for programming purposes. The department may have to be transformed into a more generalized and inclusive term such as a planning unit.

The *planning unit* is the basic group of people and activities used for space programming. The planning unit should be of a convenient size, usually fewer than twenty people and physically unified, occupying contiguous floor space. Departments that do not meet these criteria should be reorganized for programming purposes into newly defined planning units.

Other facilities may also require an ad hoc reorganization for planning purposes. Central support functions such as a cafeteria, central supply room, shipping and receiving area, and main reception room may each be identified as a separate planning unit. Facilities that are repeated on different floors of the project such as mail rooms or coffee stations may receive a planning unit designation for each occurrence. Shared facilities such as conference rooms, file rooms, or work areas may be given separate planning unit designation rather than being arbitrarily assigned to one of the groups that shares the facility.

Once the planning units are identified, they may be coded to indicate relationships within the overall organizational structure and to facilitate entry and sorting by a computer program.

Preliminary Space Standards

Space standards refer to the square-foot area, construction, and furnishings known as the *workplace* required by each individual in the organization. Space standards may also be developed for conference rooms, file banks, or even cafeteria seating. By graphically depicting standards in the programming survey form, users can visualize each workplace and select the one that most closely matches their needs for each job function.

Although the exact size and configuration of each workplace is ultimately determined during the design phase of the project, the process is one of trial and error, and preliminary standards are typically defined at the beginning of programming. Preliminary space standards are determined by observation of existing workplace configurations and from the experience of the architect or interior designer. If the organization has a formal corporate standards program this should be used, either as stated or as a starting point for developing new or revised standards for the project.

Generally, between six and ten workplace standards for individual staff members, from the senior executive office to the desk for the file clerk, are sufficient for most projects. These standards may show walls and doors (if any) and desks, chairs, and other furniture. It may also be advantageous to show equipment, such as personal computers and electrical, data, and telephone outlets, if it is expected that these elements will be standardized for the project.

The square-foot area for a closed room or office is defined by the centerlines of the walls surrounding the room. For open workplaces or workstations there are two common methods of indicating square-foot area, each with advantages and disadvantages.

The first method is to define the open workplace by the exact *footprint* of the furniture within the workplace. Thus a 5'0" by 2'6" secretarial desk with a 3'6" typing return will have an area of 30 square feet. The primary advantage of this method is its clear, obvious logic.

One disadvantage of the footprint method is that it requires a determination before programming begins as to which workplaces are to be private offices and which are to be open workstations. If the secretarial desk in the example above were located in a private office, the square-foot area would need to increase to provide access space within the office; the room would obviously need to be larger than 30 square feet. Of course this same access space must be provided even if the workplace is in an open office area, but under the footprint method this access space is included in an overall circulation factor.

The *circulation factor* is an allowance for corridors and passageways added to the subtotal of all the workplace areas in a planning unit to arrive at the total required usable area for the planning unit. This will be discussed later in more detail. For the sake of simplicity, however, it is desirable to keep the circulation factor the same for all planning units in the project. Here is where the problem occurs. If access space to a desk is **included** in the private office definition but **excluded** from the open workstation definition, then the circulation factor for the planning units will vary depending on the percentage of workplaces that are private offices.

The solution to this dilemma is to assign an *access area* to each open plan workplace. To the secretarial desk example above, an access space of two or three feet would be indicated, thus increasing the workplace area to between 42 and 48 square feet.

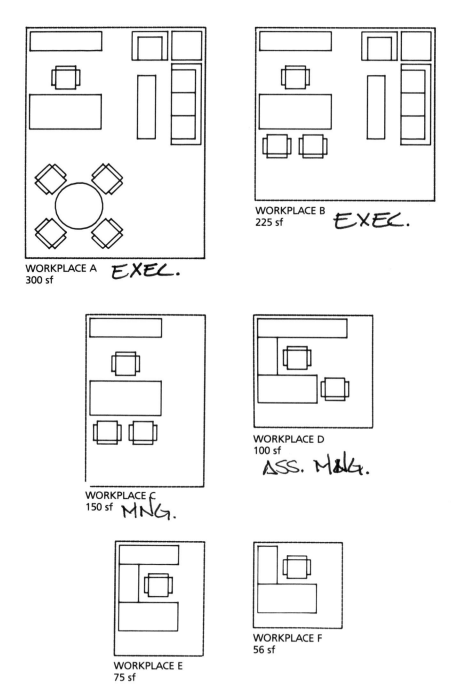

WORKPLACE A   *EXEC.*
300 sf

WORKPLACE B   *EXEC.*
225 sf

WORKPLACE C   *MNG.*
150 sf

WORKPLACE D
100 sf
ASS. MNG.

WORKPLACE E
75 sf

WORKPLACE F
56 sf

PRELIMINARY SPACE STANDARDS. During programming, space standards function as a visual reference for users. In this example, no distinction is made between closed offices and open workstations, and an allowance is made for access area.

In addition to allowing a single circulation factor to be used regardless of the mix of workplace types within planning units, this method has other advantages. It allows workplaces to be defined without reference to surrounding walls, thus postponing the decision on walls to the space planning or design phases of the project. It gives users a sense of a greater equality of size between open workstations and private offices. Finally, by minimizing the circulation factor, the appearance of greater efficiency is created.

Planning Dates

The survey form should ask for the number of workplaces required for a series of calendar dates. The first date might be the present. This acts as the benchmark and is the easiest to obtain and verify. The second date may be the date of move-in. Since most projects are built to accommodate growth for some period of time after move-in, say two to five years, a third date is usually asked for, which becomes the *planning date* for the project. It is the program for the planning date that determines how much space will be constructed and how much furniture will be purchased.

When the space program is to be used as an on-going facility management tool, many more dates—past, present, and future—may be recorded to allow for statistical tracking of growth patterns.

Survey Form Design

A planning unit *survey form* should be kept as simple as possible. There is a natural temptation to try to use a survey form to discover the most minute, subtle details about a subject. The more complex the form, however, the greater the chance for misunderstanding and the more time that must be spent in correcting errors. Written surveys are excellent

at discovering basic statistics; interviews are much better when the information is complex or technically sophisticated.

The survey form usually begins with instructions followed by an identification of the planning unit, identification of the individual completing the form, and signature lines for whatever management approvals may be required. The core of the survey is the chart of workplace types with projected numbers for the various planning dates. Workplace types includes not only offices, workstations, and desk arrangements for individual staff members, but support facilities, such as conference rooms and reception rooms and free-standing furniture, and equipment, such as copy machines and file banks, that occupy floor space within the planning unit. For clarity, separate pages may be used for "Staff Workplaces," "Support Spaces," and "Miscellaneous Files and Equipment." To assist the person completing the form, coded menus are included showing drawings of preliminary space standards.

Administering the Survey

Planning unit surveys are important documents and should receive close attention at the highest levels. The head of each planning unit should be the individual personally responsible for completing the survey form. When survey forms are complex, the project team may conduct an orientation session with the planning unit heads to explain the process. This meeting also is a good opportunity to introduce the architect or interior designer and to answer questions about the overall project.

Planning unit heads should be given about two weeks to complete their forms. Forms should be checked for completeness and obvious cases of misunderstanding and, as appropriate, sent to

SPACE REQUIREMENTS SURVEY

Project: Tyrell Corporation/Operations Center

Planning Unit: Financial Auditing

Code: 1210

Position	Type	Area	1992 Qty	Area	1994 Qty	Area	1997 Qty	Area
Director	B	225	1	225	1	225	1	225
Manager	C	150	2	300	3	450	3	450
Secretary	E	75	5	375	6	450	6	450
Sr. Auditor	D	100	12	1,200	14	1,400	14	1,400
Auditor	D	100	18	1,800	20	2,000	22	2,200
Programmers	D	100	5	500	5	500	6	600
Investigator	F	56	3	168	4	224	4	224
File Area				325		600		600
Large Conf.						450		450
Small Conf.				190		225		225
Work Area				80		120		120
Storage Area				250		400		400
				5,413		7,044		7,344
Circulation 35%				1,895		2,465		2,570
Total			46	7,308	53	9,509	56	9,914

Notes: This unit is responsible for safeguarding the company's assets and insuring that controls are implemented to minimize risk. This department should be remote from other financial departments.

By: J. S. Sebastian

Date: 8/4/—

Approved: Eldon Tyrell

Date: 8/12/—

SPACE REQUIREMENTS SURVEY. A survey form for a planning unit using three planning dates. Note the space for approvals.

other managers and executives for review and approval. Review and verification of the surveys with the planning unit heads then takes place during qualitative interviews.

QUALITATIVE INTERVIEWS

Qualitative information about an organization may be obtained through interviews. *Executive* interviews focus on corporate culture issues, growth, and organizational goals. *Operational* interviews concentrate on the primary functional activities of planning units such as work flow, privacy, security, and departmental adjacency. Finally, *special area* interviews are used to gather specific detailed requirements for facilities such as food service, telecommunications, mail rooms, and computer systems.

Interviews have a secondary objective, that of establishing credibility, cooperation, and confidence in the project design team. In addition to asking questions and recording answers, the project team must engage in a subtle marketing effort. There is a natural resistance to change that must be overcome. Ultimately a project's success is dependent on its enthusiastic acceptance by the users of the new offices. It is well to begin this process of acceptance at an early stage. Ideally, those being interviewed will emerge convinced that their personal concerns will receive thoughtful attention and that the architect or interior designer is eminently capable of providing an excellent end result.

As with all meetings, an agenda should be prepared prior to each interview. Some programmers insist that the client's project team be represented at each interview. Following the interview, meeting notes are prepared and sent to the interviewee for review and confirmation. These notes become a permanent part of the space program and are subject to approval by the organization's management.

Running through all interviews will be small asides that have little to do with the subject at hand but give insights into the client's feelings and desires. Comments such as "I really hate purple," "Smith doesn't get along with Jones," and "That red chair is very uncomfortable" should be noted or stored away in the architect's or interior designer's memory. User acceptance often depends on such small, often irrational, details. This is another reason design firms like to do their own programming.

Executive Interviews

Each executive with an interest or decision-making role in the project should be interviewed. These interviews should be conducted by the most senior members of the design team. In addition it may be desirable to interview other selected individuals to get a sampling of opinion and to encourage involvement and interest at all levels in the organization. Some of the questions that might be discussed during executive interviews include:

Project Justification: What factors generated the need for the project? Is the requirement for new facilities created by a lease expiration on existing space, outmoded existing facilities, overcrowding, or a change in geographical location to take advantage of marketing opportunities or workforce availability?

Corporate Goals and Objectives: What is the primary mission of the organization? What makes the organization unique? How does it differ from its competitors?

Management Structure: What is the management style of the organization? How does the chain of command work? How are decisions made and who makes them? How autocratic or democratic is the organization? Does the current management structure accurately reflect its needs? What changes are contemplated?

Growth: What are the growth projections for the organization? How will this be accomplished? How will these vary by department? Who prepares growth projections and what are they based on? Are there plans for decentralization, mergers, or acquisitions? How will marketing strategies affect growth and employee mix?

Technology: What is the impact of new technology on the organization? What changes are being considered? How will technology affect employee numbers, employee mix, and physical facilities? What is the schedule for introducing new systems?

Aesthetic Goals: What are the aesthetic preferences of the organization and for this particular project? What image should be projected? Is the project to be a showplace? How will issues of function, budget, and aesthetics be prioritized?

Existing Conditions: What works well in existing facilities? What doesn't work? Are there particular ideas that should be incorporated into the new project?

Confidential Information: Are there confidential plans or hidden agenda items that the design team needs to be aware of to properly design the new project? A new project means change, and change usually has an element of secrecy. (Usually this part of the discussion should not be recorded in the meeting notes.)

Operational Interviews

Operational interviews are conducted with the head of each division, department, section, and group that will occupy the new space. In addition to providing an understanding of the functional activities of each planning unit, operational interviews are an opportunity for the review and confirmation of statistical information obtained from the written surveys. Discussion questions include:

Mission: What is the function of the planning unit? How does it operate? Where does the unit fit in the overall organizational structure?

Workflow: Where does work come from? How does it arrive? What happens to it when it is here? Where does it go then?

External Adjacencies: How does the planning unit relate in terms of physical proximity to others in the organization? Which adjacencies are essential, which are desirable, and which are unwanted?

Personnel Job Functions: What are the job descriptions of individuals in the planning unit? What are their titles? How are the responsibilities of each job function accomplished in day-to-day activities?

Support Areas: What support areas such as conference rooms, coffee stations, file areas, reprographics areas, coat closets, and reception rooms are needed by the planning unit?

Internal Adjacencies: What is the optimum physical arrangement for workplaces within the planning unit? Which adjacencies are essential, which are desirable, and which are unwanted?

Privacy: What is the need for private

offices or enclosed conference rooms? Is privacy needed to preserve confidentiality, to facilitate concentration, or to indicate status? Is there a need for visual supervision of staff?

Security: Are special precautions required for safety from burglary, vandalism, or fire? Which rooms require locks? Which drawers and cabinets require locks? Are special fire resistant rooms or files required? Are vaults required?

Special Situations: Are there shift workers, job-sharing arrangements, temporary employees, or summer interns? Are there employees who are in remote locations, work at home, or who are out of the office most of the time? Are there offices that should be shared by several employees? Are there facilities that could or should be shared with other planning units?

Special Facility Interviews

Special facility interviews are conducted with the manager of each facility plus technical personnel with expertise regarding the particular system. On the design team side, engineers or other consultants may be added. General questions to be asked of all include the adequacy of existing facilities, required size of the new facility, lead time for ordering equipment, the need for special consultants, and the role manufacturers or vendors are expected to play in the layout or design of the new facility. Typical special facilities include:

Computer Systems: Will a main-frame computer facility be required? How large a room will be needed? What will be the electrical, air conditioning, structural, and cabling requirements? Is an uninterrupted power source or special fire suppressant system needed? Which employ-ees will have terminals or personal computers? Is a raised floor desirable?

Food Service: What is the extent of food service to be provided? Will there be executive dining, an employee cafeteria, vending machines, and coffee stations? What will the menu include and what kitchen facilities will be required? How many people will be served at one time and how many seatings will there be for each meal? How will food be dispensed? What will be the bussing procedure? What should be the design character or ambience of each food service facility?

Reprographics: Is a central reprographics facility required? What will be its capacity and what kind of work will be done? How does work arrive and how is the finished product distributed? Are there decentralized copy areas? Will personal copiers be provided? How is reprographics related to word processing or computer systems?

Telecommunications: What system will be used? What are the structural, electrical, cabling, and air conditioning needs of the system? What rooms and distribution closets will be required, and what will be their size and capacity? How is the telecommunications system integrated with the computer system? What equipment will be located at each workplace? Where will facsimile transmission devices be located? How are future additions and revisions to be accommodated?

Mail and Messenger Service: Is there to be a central mail room and how large will it be? Will there be decentralized mail areas? How are mail and messages received, processed, and delivered?

File Areas: What is the volume and type

of filing anticipated? What type of equipment will be used, such as file cabinets, shelving, compact systems, or electronic systems? How are files opened, received, processed, accessed, distributed, and controlled? What file room staff is required and what kind of workstations do they need? Will a purge program be implemented before the move? Will off-site dead filing be used?

Audio-Visual Facilities: What type of audio-visual equipment will be used in conference rooms or other areas? Will dedicated classrooms be needed, and how will they be equipped? Will an auditorium be required? Will video-teleconferencing be required, and what type of studio set-up will be needed? What will be the audio-visual capability of the board room? What will be the acoustical criteria for the various areas?

Supplies: Will there be a central supply room? Will there be satellite supply areas? What is the required capacity of each area? How do supplies enter the building, and how are they received and distributed? What is the supply room staff, and what kinds of workstations are required? What facilities will be required for recycling programs?

Libraries: How large are libraries to be, and where should they be located? What types of materials are kept in the library, such as books, reports, periodicals, video tapes, computer tapes, or printouts? What size shelving is required? What will be the lighting, structural, and acoustical requirements? Who accesses the library and how? Are study carrels, lounge areas, or conference rooms required? What type of security or control will be required? What will be the extent of microfilming or other equip-

ment? What facilities will be needed for the library staff?

Artwork: Is there a corporate artwork program? How is the artwork budget determined? Who selects and places artwork? How is artwork allocated to private offices, open work areas, and other spaces?

Security: Will special security be required and why? Will twenty-four-hour or overnight security be required? What areas must be secure and to what extent? Are guards required? Where will they be located, and what facilities will they require? What electronic surveillance will be used?

Maintenance: Will the facility be maintained by in-house staff, the building owner, or outside contractor? What facilities, such as janitor's closets, workshops, or locker rooms, will be required?

PROGRAM ANALYSIS

At the conclusion of the information-gathering phase of project programming, the project team assembles and analyzes the data and prepares the *final program* document. There are many ways to organize and present programming data. The goal is clarity and simplicity; understanding by the client and usefulness to the design team.

Typical steps in organizing and analyzing statistical information include:

Verification of planning unit designations. There should be no gaps in the organization chart; everyone should be counted but no one counted twice.

Verification that the survey forms are complete and the mathematics accurate. Generally there will be errors and misunderstandings on some of the forms and return visits to some of the planning unit heads will be necessary.

Verification that survey forms have been reviewed and approved at the appropriate levels in the chain of command.

Verification of growth rates. Different managers may have different approaches to organizational growth. Some will minimize growth to show frugality; others will maximize growth to show optimism and aggressiveness. The architect or interior designer should attempt to insure consistency and realism in growth projections and question projections that seem out of line.

Resolution of inconsistencies in the assignment of workplace standards. Similar job functions and titles should be assigned similar workplaces in all planning units.

Once there is agreement that the raw data is complete and correct, a *circulation factor* is added to the net workplace area of each planning unit to arrive at the total net floor space needed by each planning unit. A circulation factor is a percentage added to net workplace area to allow for corridors and passageways within the planning unit.

A circulation factor is a statistical abstraction and its determination is a judgment call. Great precision in selecting a circulation factor is not only unnecessary but impossible. An area variation of from 5 to 10 percent between what is selected and what is finally designed is within a reasonable contingency range. Any attempt at greater precision will usually result in constricting the space planning and design process.

It is generally desirable to standardize on one circulation factor for the entire project although for planning units made up primarily of large, bulk spaces, such as storage rooms, a lower factor may be used than for typical office space. If desired, executive areas may be allowed a larger circulation factor.

There are several ways of determining a reasonable circulation factor for the project. The first is experience. Circulation factors don't vary greatly between similar projects and experience on past projects is usually a good preliminary guide. A second way is to analyze the existing office space. This may be quickly done by measuring the overall existing area for several planning units, subtracting existing workplace area, and calculating the existing circulation area. A third method is to prepare quick hypothetical space plan studies for the new space and calculate the resulting factor.

A typical circulation factor for office space is in the range of 25 to 40 percent. This is usually satisfactory for planning units when open workplaces are defined to include an access area.

If the footprint method is used in defining workplace standards, the circulation factor will vary depending on the proportion of workplaces that are closed rooms versus those in open areas. Planning units with primarily private offices and closed rooms will still be in the 25 to 40 percent range. However, totally open planning under this method may require a circulation factor of 60 to 75 percent.

When the required area of each planning unit has been determined, the total net area for the project may be calculated. This generally does **not** include the primary circulation on the floor of a building. Primary floor circulation that provides access to the elevator lobby, toilet rooms, and fire stairs may add another 5 to 10 percent to total net area to arrive at a total usable area for the project.

Space programming does not usually deal with rentable area, which may add an additional 15 to 30 percent to total required usable area depending on the terms of the lease.

THE ADJACENCY SEQUENCE

There is a logical progression from a company's organization chart to the space plan. This progression might be called the adjacency sequence. It begins with an organization chart, perhaps with the familiar pyramid configuration, continues through an adjacency matrix, bubble diagram, scaled adjacency diagram, block plan, and stack diagram, and ends with the space layout. Each procedure in the transformation takes the project one step away from an abstract reflection of a hierarchical reporting structure and one step closer to a realization of that structure in physical office space.

Although it is common to combine some steps in the procedure, the activities required for each step must be done in some fashion for all projects. From a contractual standpoint, some steps in the adjacency sequence may be part of the programming phase and some may be included with schematic design. The pro-cess forms the link between the two phases, and the demarcation point may be somewhat arbitrary.

The adjacency sequence may be performed at several levels. Overall charts and diagrams show relationships between planning units. Adjacency sequences may also be developed within planning units to study working relationships between individuals.

Computer programs, often integrated with CADD software, are available to perform many types of adjacency studies. These can save time in manipulating large amounts of mathematical data but may produce bizarre results unless tempered by the subjective ingenuity of the architect or interior designer. A well-conceived block or stack diagram, solving qualitative as well as quantitative concerns, is a creative exercise.

Organization Chart

The *organization chart* is prepared by the client and given to the design firm as background information. This chart shows the hierarchical reporting relation-

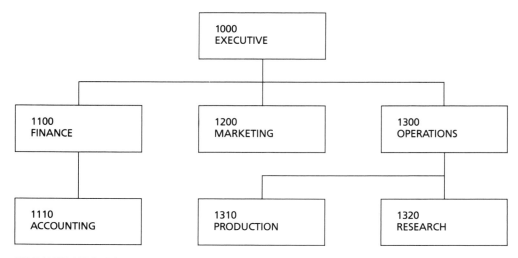

ORGANIZATION CHART. A typical corporate organization chart prepared by a client and given to the architect or interior designer.

ships of the company. For large projects, there will be a series of charts with a master organization chart showing overall departmental relationships and departmental charts showing the reporting relationships of individuals within each department. The charts should be current with a code and consistent nomenclature for each department and for individuals identified by both name and title. The departments and individuals to be included in the project should be clearly identified. Information on the organization charts should be confirmed during the operational and executive interviews.

Adjacency Matrix

Organization charts say a great deal about reporting relationships but nothing about physical adjacency requirements. They do not say, for example, that although an accounting clerk may report to a supervisor on the twenty-third floor, he or she must sit next to a production clerk on the third floor. Step two in the sequence is the gathering of adjacency information; determining the physical location relationships of planning units that will maximize workflow.

The most efficient way to obtain this information is on the survey forms, followed by confirmation during executive and operational interviews. Each planning unit head should be asked about the optimum workflow adjacency to every other planning unit. Sometimes this is done by asking the respondent to list the planning units that must be located close by and to list the planning units where work product comes from and the planning units where work product goes.

A more complete picture may be obtained by a coding system. For each level of adjacency a code may be assigned and survey respondents may be asked to use this code to indicate the desired level of adjacency with each of the other planning units in the organization. Five levels of adjacency are usually sufficient, such as essential, important, desirable, none, and undesirable.

The code results may be entered into an *adjacency matrix*. For each matrix intersection there will, of course, be two sources, one from each of the respective planning unit heads. Where both sources agree, the agreed code is entered. Where the sources disagree, the cause of the disagreement should be investigated and concurrence reached.

A raw adjacency matrix, perhaps organized alphabetically or by a corporate coding system, will have adjacency codes distributed in an almost random way. To increase its usefulness, a game, a sort of

1	2	1	5	1	1	1200 MARKETING
2	2	2	3	5		1110 ACCOUNTING
2	1	2	5			1100 FINANCE
2	3	4				1000 EXECUTIVE
5	5					1300 OPERATIONS
4						1320 RESEARCH

1310 PRODUCTION

CODE:
5 Essential Adjacency
4 Important Adjacency
3 Desirable Adjacency
2 No Adjacency Requirement
1 Adjacency Is Undesirable

ADJACENCY MATRIX. The physical adjacency requirements of every pair of departments is given a numerical value from 5 (essential) to 1 (unnecessary or undesirable). These adjacencies are entered into the matrix. If planning units are reordered to concentrate high values to the right side of the matrix, a pattern of clusters of planning units that should be located together will begin to emerge.

trial-and-error exercise to group planning units according to adjacency requirements, may be played. The purpose of the game is to locate planning units with essential relationships close to each other on the chart and those with undesirable relationships far apart. This is done by rearranging planning units in the chart so that high code numbers will be close to the front edge of the chart and low numbers located at the far end. The result will be a linear organizational listing with planning units with high adjacency requirements clustered together. This will begin to tell the architect or interior designer how planning units ought to be physically located in the office layout.

Bubble Diagram

Matrix diagrams are one-dimensional and this is their limitation. A single floor plan is two-dimensional, and offices on many floors of a building form a three-dimensional arrangement. Step three of the adjacency sequence begins to solve

this dilemma by the creation of a *bubble diagram*. In a typical bubble diagram each planning unit is indicated by an identically sized geometric shape. Adjacencies are indicated by locating the bubbles with high adjacency requirements close to each other and by indicating the adjacency by the thickness of the line connecting the bubbles. Like the matrix, the bubble diagram is a trial-and-error game, and several attempts may be necessary until a logical result is obtained.

Scaled Adjacency Diagram

The primary value of bubble diagrams for both client and design firm is that they show in an abstract but very graphic and understandable way the spatial relationships that will be realized in the final office layout. They do not, however, show size. Large departments and small departments, large private offices and small workstations, are all shown with same-sized bubbles. Step four then is to take the departmental and workplace size requirements from the survey forms

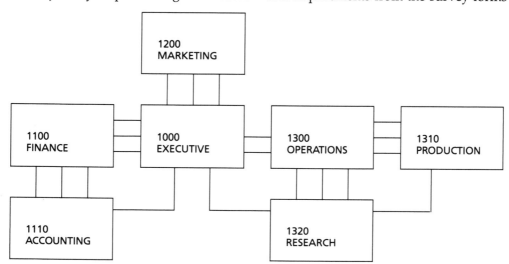

BUBBLE DIAGRAM. Each rectangle represents a planning unit. Lines between rectangles indicate adjacency levels. The diagram may be manipulated so that planning units with the highest adjacency values are closest together.

and combine them with the bubble diagram to create a *scaled adjacency diagram*. Sometimes a scaled adjacency diagram is nothing more than a bubble diagram with circles drawn to scale. Further refinements may be made. The bubbles can become rectangles, and the lines between can be organized to suggest pathways. A beautifully drawn scaled adjacency diagram almost looks like a space plan without a building and can be a powerful tool in assisting the client in understanding the relationship between program and physical office space.

Block Plan

Step five is to combine the scaled adjacency diagram with the floor plan of the building. For each floor of the building a *block plan* may be developed. The block plan shows the planning units, indicated as rectangles drawn to scale, arranged on the floor. The rectangles should be logically placed in the plan with due regard to desired interior or perimeter locations, optimum relationships to the building

core and elevator lobby, and consideration for the location of potential corridors between planning units.

The first thing that will become apparent is that the total required programmed area of the planning units will never exactly match the occupiable area available on the floor. Further, planning units will never fit neatly into logical building modules. To reconcile these differences, the concept of *assigned area* may be used. Rather than shoehorning required area to match space available, planning units are given assigned areas on the floor that approximate the required areas but that relate to the building module in some logical way. Required area and assigned area are then tracked in parallel with the differences noted.

Since both required areas and assigned areas inevitably contain statistical errors in the range of 5 to 10 percent, differences within this range should not ultimately affect space planning. If total required area on a floor is greater than available usable area by more than 10 percent, the

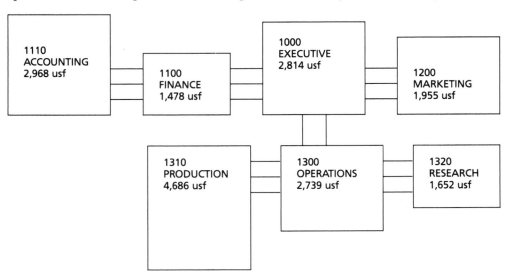

SCALED ADJACENCY DIAGRAM. A scaled adjacency diagram is a version of a bubble diagram with the "bubbles" drawn to scale.

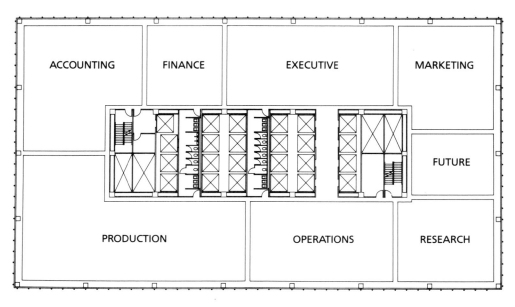

		REQUIRED AREA	ASSIGNED AREA
1000	Executive	2,814 usf	3,000 usf
1100	Finance	1,478	1,400
1110	Accounting	2,968	3,000
1200	Marketing	1,955	2,200
1300	Operations	2,730	2,600
1310	Production	4,686	4,800
1320	Research	1,652	1,800
	Future	0	1,200
Total/Floor 4		18,283 usf	20,000 usf

BLOCK PLAN. Planning units are located on the floor in accordance with adjacency requirements. Assigned area relates closely to required area and is consistent with the building module.

block planning should be reevaluated and reassignments made. Conversely, significant space left over may be assigned as "future."

Stack Diagram

Where the project will occupy more than one floor in a building, a vertical section known as a *stack diagram* may be cut through the building to show the relationship between floors. A stack diagram resembles a bar chart. Each floor of the building is shown with the length of the bar corresponding to the available usable area of the floor. The assigned area of each planning unit is shown by shaded areas of different lengths within the bar. The amount of space over or under becomes clearly visible.

The stack diagram is useful in the determination of desirable expansion or option space. By showing an entire multi-floor project in one view, relationships that cannot easily be displayed in any other way become dramatically apparent. The stack diagram is the most subjective, qualitative step in the adjacency sequence. It usually attracts the greatest client interest and is generally the one most studied and revised.

The final step in the adjacency sequence is *space planning*. This must wait until the schematic design phase of the project.

PRESENTATION OF
THE SPACE PROGRAM

The space program is an important document, signifying, in a contractual sense, the completion of the programming phase. It is also the first opportunity for the architect or interior designer to present a formal work product on the project to the client. The report should be logically organized and graphically attractive. It may begin with a summary of conclusions followed by a discussion of method-

ology, assumptions, and a description of preliminary standards. The heart of the report consists of a narrative discussing qualitative issues and conclusions, the planning unit personnel, workplace and area requirements, and adjacencies illustrated in block and stack diagrams.

After a verbal presentation of the report, the client should be requested to review and give formal *written approval* so that work may begin on the schematic design phase. Sometimes clients are reluctant to sign the document, feeling that they are thus prevented from making any changes. It must be explained that change is still possible, indeed inevitable, but that it must be controlled through a formal process of authorization and approval and that there may be schedule and fee implications.

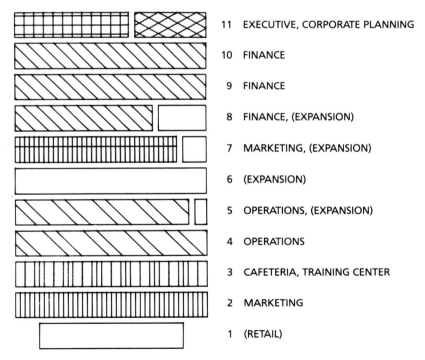

11 EXECUTIVE, CORPORATE PLANNING

10 FINANCE

9 FINANCE

8 FINANCE, (EXPANSION)

7 MARKETING, (EXPANSION)

6 (EXPANSION)

5 OPERATIONS, (EXPANSION)

4 OPERATIONS

3 CAFETERIA, TRAINING CENTER

2 MARKETING

1 (RETAIL)

STACK DIAGRAM. This is a stack diagram for a full building project showing the vertical arrangement of major divisions of the client's organization. Future expansion areas are also located.

CHAPTER SIX

BUDGETS AND
SCHEDULES

Budgets and schedules are the framework within which a project is conceived and implemented. They define the limits. More than most project types, office design is sensitive to the implications of budgets and schedules. The function of office space is to improve the operations of a profit-making organization. Cost overruns may directly affect the company's bottom line, and missed schedules can result in severe lease penalties and operational difficulties.

Budgeting and scheduling are not direct project activities, such as drawing a detail or constructing a partition. Theoretically a project could be completed without a budget or a schedule. It is a great temptation for a project manager to put off the preparation or updating of these project controls to attend to supposedly more urgent tasks. These are activities that when conscientiously pursued can yield enormous benefits, but if done sporadically and carelessly they can be a waste of time.

Once developed, budgets and schedules should be reviewed and revised regularly. There should be permanent line items for project controls on every agenda of every client and project meeting. The question should be asked: "What has happened since the last meeting that will affect time and money?" Almost every change or refinement in the project will have budget and schedule implications that must be considered in the decision-making process.

Budgets and schedules are moving targets. They constantly change in response to new developments. To say that a project "met the budget" or "was finished on time" is meaningful only in the sense that the budget and schedule were kept constantly under control, not that they achieved an initial, perhaps arbitrary, goal. The final cost and occupancy date may bear no relationship to those established initially, but if they reflect an organized and responsible process, the project may be considered a success.

The great temptation in budget and schedule preparation is wishful thinking. Since both the design firm and client want to put as much into the project as they can afford and allow themselves as much time as possible, there is a natural human tendency to be overly optimistic. What they may fail to realize is that each line or line item is an accumulation of data from a great number of sources, each of whom may also want to give their "best price" or "best date." A construction commencement date, for example, may depend on contractor availability, drawing completion, the issue of a building permit, and numerous client and landlord approvals. Similarly, the cost of a door may involve prices from seven or eight subcontractors and suppliers, as well as a general contractor. With so many players all hoping for the best, it is virtually impossible to expect that all will come through as predicted, and inevitably the budget or schedule will be exceeded.

To protect against this optimism as well as variations in the marketplace and to provide a cushion for the unexpected, it is normal to include a contingency in budgets and schedules. A typical budget contingency is 10 percent. Scheduling contingencies are generally not formalized in this way but should be included just the same.

If further objectivity is required, it may be brought by a construction manager, a furniture project manager, a scheduling consultant, or cost consultant. A construction manager may have broad responsibilities on a project, one of which is usually the preparation and maintenance of the construction schedule and budget. Similarly, one of the duties of a furniture project manager may be assistance with the furnishings schedule. Cost and scheduling consultants' roles are more limited. Under the quantity surveyor concept imported from England, a cost consultant's sole responsibility is advising the client of expected costs based on the drawings and other documents.

Consulting on project schedules is a

relatively new specialty. The expertise of scheduling consultants relies upon their manipulation of complex computer programs.

The advantage of these outside consultants is their objectivity. They have no vested interest in optimizing the budgets or schedules. On the contrary, their motivation is to be as pessimistic as possible. Their success is based solely on the schedules and budgets being met, not the end product itself. Instead of best-case, they will be looking at worst-case scenarios.

PROJECT BUDGETS

Every client has a mental image of what a given project should cost. This may be a vague intuitive guess or a detailed lump-sum or square-footage estimate. Along with a cost estimate, every client has a vision of what the project will look like. It is the architect's or interior designer's responsibility to reconcile the cost with the vision, to assist the client in assessing the financial feasibility of the project. This is accomplished by the preparation of the *project budget*.

A budget sets the quality and complexity level of a project. It helps the client determine and justify funds allocated or borrowed for the project. As work proceeds, the budget tracks the development, refinement, and change in the project. It helps the architect or interior designer and client choose between design alternatives. Finally it assists in tracking contractor and supplier bids and estimates.

Even after the budget has been prepared it may still be difficult for the client to thoroughly understand and visualize the relationship between cost and expectations. What will fifty dollars per square foot buy? A hundred? One hundred and fifty?

There is a "chicken and egg" element in this dilemma. Design should not begin until the budget is established, and yet it is difficult to know what a project will cost until it is designed.

Architects and interior designers attempt to solve this problem in several ways. Budgeting by ranges—low, medium and high—with a written description of the extent of construction and furnishings each range will accommodate is one method. Another solution is to show plans and photographs of past projects with indications of cost ranges. The danger of this approach is that the client may fix on specific aesthetic solutions that are inappropriate for the project.

Each phase of a project should include a budgeting or estimating activity. Technically, a budget is a goal, established by the client as a statement of what he or she is willing to pay. An estimate, on the other hand, is based on a take-off of actual items and quantities. A bid is an offer by a contractor or vendor to provide a particular item for a specific amount of money. A price is a contracted amount. It is important to keep these distinctions in mind, even though in practice they form a continuum. Beginning with a broad-brush idea of what the project should cost, the costing procedure moves step by step through the phases and from budget to estimate to bid to price; ever more detailed and refined, culminating in actual payments to contractors and vendors.

Initial Budget

Responsibility for project costs should be clearly established in the professional service contract. Typically, the client is responsible for preparing the *initial project budget* that is presented to the architect or interior designer during the programming phase. The design professional is responsible for advising the client as to the adequacy of the budget for the accomplishment of the project.

Often the preparation of the initial budget may be beyond the technical capabilities of the client, so the architect or interior designer may be asked to assist in its preparation. This assistance does not relieve the client of responsibility for the budget.

In format the initial budget may show lump-sum or square-footage allowances for various components of the work, such as general construction, carpeting, and furniture, and for various types of space, such as executive suites, computer areas, clerical departments, and food service facilities. It should include a percentage contingency, perhaps 10 percent.

Schematic Design Phase Budget

In the schematic design phase the architect or interior designer is responsible for updating the initial budget in light of recommended design concepts, using current projects of similar scope and quality as a benchmark. Anticipated costs in a *schematic design budget* are usually stated on a cost per square foot basis. Even though reflective of space planning results, the schematic design phase budget still represents a goal rather than a calculation of anything already determined. Nevertheless, the budget should be as detailed as possible in its description of the qualitative scope of the work.

Design Development Phase Estimate

In the design development phase a budget becomes more of an estimate as it is further refined to reflect the detailed development of the design. It becomes more complex and shows expected quantities and estimated unit costs.

Contract Document Phase Estimate

Additional revision may occur during the preparation of contract documents. These refinements may be based on

PRELIMINARY BUDGET

Prepared for the Nakasone Corporation based on the Program Report dated 12/10/—.

	Rentable Area	Unit Cost	Total Cost
GENERAL CONSTRUCTION			
Executive	16,385	$150	$2,457,750
Corporate Planning	7,345	110	807,950
Finance	63,845	60	3,830,700
Marketing	42,940	110	4,723,400
Operations	44,353	60	2,661,150
Cafeteria and Kitchen	15,481	200	3,096,200
Training Center	7,119	60	427,140
Lobby Upgrade (Allow)			400,000
			18,404,290
Workletter Allowance	197,468	(26)	(5,134,155)
Subtotal/Construction			13,270,135
FURNISHINGS			
Furniture	197,468	50	9,873,400
Carpeting	197,468	5	987,340
Graphics (Allow)			200,000
Artwork (Allow)			350,000
Audio-visual (Allow)			240,000
Moving Expenses	197,468	2	394,936
Subtotal/Furnishings			12,045,676
Subtotal			25,315,811
Contingency		10%	2,531,581
Total	197,468	$141	$27,847,392

Not Included:

Architectural, interior design, and other consultant fees
Telecommunications and computer equipment costs

PRELIMINARY BUDGET. A preliminary budget, prepared during the programming phase, represents a target based on square foot costs of similar projects.

PRELIMINARY ESTIMATE OF CONSTRUCTION COSTS

Prepared for the Nakasone Corporation based on Scheme 2B for Floor 4, dated 2/4/—.

	Quantity		Unit Cost	Total Cost
1. Partitions/interior	1,678	lf	48.00	80,544
Partitions/acoustic	148	lf	68.00	10,064
Partitions/glass	220	lf	550.00	121,000
2. Doors/interior	35	ea	1,150.00	40,250
Doors/glass entry	2	pr	6,000.00	12,000
3. Ceilings/acoustical	20,000	sf	4.50	90,000
4. Wall finish/paint	19,500	sf	0.60	11,700
Wall finish/fabric	650	sf	4.50	2,925
5. Millwork/counters	120	lf	200.00	24,000
Millwork/shelving	240	lf	425.00	102,000
6. Carpet	2,300	yd	45.00	103,500
Resilient tile	600	sf	2.50	1,500
7. Mechanical/allow	20,000	sf	16.50	330,000
8. Electrical/allow	20,000	sf	11.50	230,000
9. Sprinklers	20,000	sf	1.50	30,000
Plumbing/coffee	4	ea	3,500.00	14,000
Subtotal				1,203,483
General Conditions and Fee			20%	240,697
Total/General Construction				1,444,180
Cost/RSF	22,600	rsf		$63.90

Not Included:

Architectural, interior design, and other consultant fees
Furnishings
Telecommunications and computers equipment costs

PRELIMINARY ESTIMATE. This example shows an estimate of construction costs developed from a preliminary space plan. Unit costs at this stage are rough averages and do not represent specific materials selections.

informal discussions with contractors and vendors, price lists and expected discounts for furnishings, and knowledge of current market conditions. The final design estimate prepared before the issue of contract documents to contractors and vendors should be expected to accurately reflect the anticipated cost of the project within a reasonable contingency range.

Budget Categories

Construction budgets may be thought of in three categories: building standard costs, required budget, and discretionary expenses. The building standard budget is the minimum construction cost required for occupancy by a *typical* tenant. It includes building standard quality and quantity of ceilings, lighting, partitions, doors, heating, ventilating, and air conditioning (HVAC) work, electrical work, fire protection sprinklers, floor covering, and window covering. Not included are furnishings, special HVAC, special lighting or other electrical work, or decorative finishes and cabinetwork. The significance of the building standard budget is that it is often included in the lease package offered by the landlord. It may be an important part of lease negotiations, and the client should fully understand what will be provided.

The *required budget* category includes, in addition to building standard work, items of construction necessary to meet the particular occupancy requirements of the client. These may include special lighting, HVAC, electrical, plumbing, or structural requirements necessary for office operations, code required items not provided as building standard, work required for computer or telecommunications installation, and any additional or special partitioning, doors, or other items, such as acoustical treatment. This is the budget that sets a fixed minimum

to the cost of the project. Because different buildings have different capabilities to accommodate these special tenant requirements, a required budget may be prepared for each competing site for comparison purposes. Landlords or their on-site design firms or contractors are often willing to prepare these budgets for prospective tenants. These budgets should be independently verified.

The *discretionary budget* includes the decorative items that will give the offices their special character. Typically this includes special ceilings and lighting, special wall coverings, paneling, cabinetwork, sophisticated detailing of partitioning and doors, interconnecting stairs, special flooring of wood, stone, or tile, built-in equipment, and plumbing for lunchrooms and private bathrooms. This budget may vary from zero to several hundred dollars per square foot. Discretionary costs usually may be assumed to be roughly the same in any building selected and thus need not be a factor in site comparison.

Furnishings budgets are generally less complicated than construction budgets. Since furnishings are usually manufactured items with price lists, accurate budget information is readily available. To budget or estimate a furnishings item, one takes the list price, multiplies by an appropriate discount expected from a manufacturer or dealer, and adds a factor for transportation and installation. A difficulty in furnishings budgeting arises in tracking the number of items involved and the seemingly infinite combinations and permutations in sizes, components, and finishes.

Budget Limitations

It should be clearly understood by the client that while the design team may prepare a budget, it cannot guarantee or be responsible for actual bids or costs proposed by contractors or vendors. There is a limit to the accuracy that a design professional may be expected to bring to budget preparation due to marketplace variables. General market conditions, competitive pressures, management efficiencies, and variations in expected profit margins by contractors and vendors can significantly affect costs in ways that are totally beyond the control of architects and interior designers. The only ones who can quote costs with precision are those who will actually supply the goods and receive payment. Since competitive bids between contractors, who work from detailed documents and stake their futures on the result, can vary by 10 to 20 percent, it is hard to see how design professionals can be expected to be more accurate.

Budgets have different meanings to different clients. For some clients such as professional service organizations and privately held companies the budget may be considered a desirable goal. While the design firm is expected to work within the approved budget, the budget may be increased with appropriate justification.

On the other hand, budgets for large corporate projects may be fixed by corporate authorization and may be increased only after reconsideration of the entire project. Obviously this puts serious pressure on the architect or interior designer, as well as on the facility manager or other corporate representative responsible for the budget. In these cases great care should be given to providing an adequate contingency in the initial authorization request.

All budgets must be as clear about what is **not** included as well as what is included. Total costs for a project include many other things besides construction,

furnishings, and design fees. Such items as moving expenses, telecommunications costs, new office equipment, building assessments, taxes, interest, and even allowances for lost employee time are all real costs of an office move, and different organizations account for these in different ways. The decision as to what is to be included and what omitted from the budget should be clearly understood by both the design firm and the client. Often this is established by corporate custom or determined by a consideration of tax consequences.

PROJECT SCHEDULING

There is a particular urgency about office projects. There never seems to be enough time to design and build a project the way it should be done. This is partly because business growth and change occur faster than the time it takes to build facilities, partly because leases are written with too little time for design and construction before rent commences, and partly because new office space is often not high on the list of management priorities.

For the facility manager, architect, and interior designer, it would be convenient if management would delay hiring additional staff and postpone the introduction of a new product or service for a year or two until the design and construction of new offices can be accomplished at a thoughtful pace. In the real world this doesn't happen very often. An office is not an end in itself. Its purpose is to support the primary mission of the company. As such its design and construction must respond to the needs of the organization, not the other way around.

To design and build an office in a timely fashion requires scheduling—a fundamental management task with the purpose of planning, predicting, and tracking project activities. A schedule portrays the relationships and sequences between tasks indicating which tasks must be completed before new ones may be started. It indicates how tasks may be overlapped or phased to save time.

A schedule has no inherent value in and of itself. By itself, a schedule cannot reduce the time it takes to do a task by one minute. Just because a schedule is prepared does not mean that the project will be completed on time. A schedule's sole value lies in the information it provides for decision making.

Schedules can never be considered final; they are constantly changed by new information. The success of a scheduling process is not how closely the actual work matches the initial schedule, but how well the schedule responds to project change while still meeting overall project objectives. An effective schedule must be periodically checked and updated.

Effective scheduling is based on the concept that the sooner a problem is identified, the easier it will be to solve. Possibly the most important function of a schedule is as an early warning device. A schedule can provide a forceful reminder when a project is in trouble and remedial action is required. This is commonly done by periodically checking actual progress against expected progress. Paradoxically this is where many scheduling efforts break down. Either the schedule is so complex that the trouble spots are hard to find in the maze of detail or the project manager becomes too busy with other things to spend the time required to check and update the schedule. When this happens this management tool becomes nothing more than a pretty wall decoration giving a false sense of security.

Scheduling can help in project definition. A project expected to be completed in five months will be approached differently from one with a two-year time frame. Construction will be less complex, and materials and furnishings may be limited to what is readily available.

Unfortunately this realization sometimes happens too late. There are many examples of companies, without a real understanding of design and construction time requirements, signing leases that require occupancy in a few short months while still expecting elaborate cabinetwork and exotic furnishings. The architect or interior designer is then faced with the unhappy task of reconciling these design expectations with an impossible schedule.

Among the benefits of careful scheduling is the assurance that the proper design staff will be available to contribute to the project at the proper time. Whether it is the principal who should be available Friday afternoons at three o'clock for project review, or the draftsperson who will be required in six weeks for a two month period, scheduling allows individuals to plan their work, make time available, and be mentally prepared when the time comes.

A schedule provides encouragement for decision making. There is a strong human tendency to put off making a decision as long as possible. Parkinson's law states that "work will expand to fulfill the time allotted for its completion." A schedule identifies that completion date—the point at which a decision must be made.

The client's effect on a project schedule should not be underestimated. Significant time is consumed by client reviews and approvals as well as requests for restudy and revision. Responsibility for meeting a project schedule rests as much on the client as it does on the design professionals and contractors. Client deadlines should be just as carefully established and rigorously enforced.

Schedules may be used to establish and justify design fees, which are basically a reflection of the number of hours spent by the project team. As a graphic depiction of those hours, the schedule can assist the project manager in determining how many people will be required, and for what time period, for each phase and task on the project.

Fast-Track Scheduling

When establishing project goals, time is one factor that must take its place in a priority list along with cost, quality, operational efficiency, and so on. If speed is high on the list, *fast-track scheduling* techniques may be appropriate. This requires breaking the project into separate, out-of-sequence tracks and scheduling "just-in-time" delivery of design, documents, materials, construction work, and furnishings for each. Since work on each track proceeds independently, the overall project schedule may be compressed.

The breakdown into separate tracks is typically by construction trade. Rather than waiting until documentation is complete for the entire project for bidding to contractors for a lump-sum price, packages are issued by trade as documents are completed and as they occur in the construction sequence, beginning with mechanical, electrical, and ceiling work and concluding with finishes, carpeting, and furnishings.

Fast-track scheduling usually means retaining the services of a construction manager and possibly a furniture project manager during the design phases of the project. Their first task is to identify long lead time items so that these may be selected and ordered early. Document production is sequenced so that as each trade section is completed, it is bid to subcontractors, and then work commences. Ceiling and partition construction may be

proceeding simultaneously with design work on cabinetwork and finishes.

A version of fast-track scheduling is often practiced with great sophistication in new buildings where the owner provides basic interior construction under a workletter. By prestocking many construction items, such as drywall, light fixtures, door frames, hardware, and ceilings, and by streamlining the pricing and approval process, dates for move-in and rent commencement may be accelerated.

Fast-track scheduling requires increased management time in coordinating a series of separate schedules and increased design time in producing separate documents and documents out of normal project sequence.

Although fast-track scheduling may speed project delivery, there are disadvantages that should be considered. During the design phases, decisions must be made more quickly based on fewer options. Drawings may not be as thoroughly checked and more errors may be expected. Early decisions may need to be changed due to later developments. Construction work may cost more due to overtime work and expedited deliveries. Mistakes in the field may increase. Furniture selections may be limited to in-stock programs or to items with relatively short lead times. Customization may be limited. Clients must be willing to accept the substitution of products, even if more expensive, if the lead time is shorter.

Phased Schedules

Phased schedules break a project down by location rather than by trade. This may be appropriate when projects are so large that documentation and construction are most efficiently performed in smaller increments, usually floor-by-floor. Phasing may also be necessary for remodeling projects where client operations cannot be interrupted by construction work. In this situation client departments may move in 'round robin fashion—first into swing space, then to the final remodeled location.

Phasing usually begins after the overall design concept has been presented and approved. Based on the concept, final space planning and documentation proceeds on a floor-by-floor basis. As documents for each floor or group of floors are completed, they are bid to general contractors or bid to subcontractors by the construction manager. Construction progresses in the same order. When construction is complete and furnishings installed, client move-in occurs and work begins again on the next area.

Phasing has many of the same disadvantages of fast-track scheduling. Its primary advantage is that very large or complex projects are divided into a series of subprojects more easily managed by design professionals, contractors, and clients alike.

Schedule Formats

The simplest form of schedule is the *narrative schedule* or task list. A task list includes a short description of a task, the date when it is expected to be completed, and an identification of the responsible party. What it lacks is a visualization of the sequences and relationships between tasks. As such it has limited use for an overall project. It may be extremely useful, however, in short-term task identification and assignment, tracking project problems, and encouraging decision making.

The most common schedule format is the *bar chart*. In developing a bar chart schedule, the entire project is divided into discrete tasks and a duration determined for each. A start date for each task is established. The tasks are then listed in chronological order on a graph with a line, or bar, drawn to indicate the start date and duration of each task. Benchmark activities, events such as presentations or approvals that have no duration, may be indicated by a symbol.

The number of tasks and events listed on a bar chart will depend on when the schedule is prepared, its purpose, and for whom it is intended. At the start of a project, when few details are known, the schedule may list as few as five or six tasks

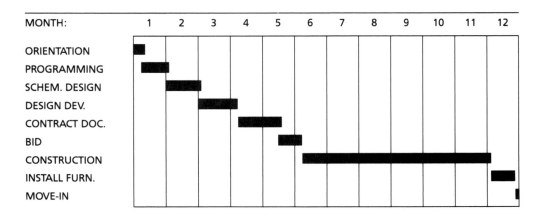

BAR CHART SCHEDULE. A bar chart schedule shows when each activity begins and ends and its duration.

corresponding to the project phases in the professional service contract. This will serve to indicate a broad overview of the project and establish the benchmark goals required to meet a final completion date.

As the project progresses, more tasks may be added, reflecting further knowledge about the project. As this is done, task durations will change and dates and sequences will be adjusted. The most detailed schedule on any project will usually be that prepared by the general contractor, which may list thousands of activities to track subcontractor progress.

The person preparing the schedule needs to be aware of the audience—those who will use it. A schedule is useful to individuals only to the extent that it can directly relate their work (and the work of those they supervise) to a larger context. Since there are various responsibility levels on a project, one schedule will seldom serve everyone's needs. Typically a project needs a series of schedules, each reflecting a different level of detail. The

client's CEO may only need a summary schedule showing major phases of work and important benchmarks; a schedule with more detail would only be confusing. Conversely, a draftsperson doing a working drawing and a mechanic in the field need a very detailed schedule, one that shows the expected work on a day-by-day, week-by-week basis.

A refinement of the bar chart schedule is the *critical path* schedule. This method requires a computer, and there are many software programs available. The purpose of critical path scheduling is to identify those tasks that, when shortened, will compress the entire schedule.

To illustrate the critical path process, two tasks may be imagined: Task A and Task B. Both may be done simultaneously but both must be completed before a third task, Task C, can be started. Task A will take five days, while Task B will have a duration of three days. The total time before Task C can start is therefore five days—the time it takes to complete

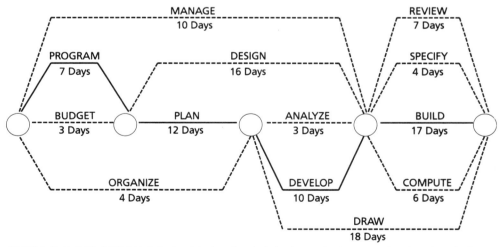

CRITICAL PATH SCHEDULE. A critical path schedule shows the duration of each task and when it can begin based on the completion of prior tasks. The critical path is defined as the sequence of those activities with no slack time, and a day saved on one of these activities means a day saved on the entire project. In this example the critical path is the sequence Program-Plan-Develop-Build and the minimum total required time is 46 days.

Task A. Task B will be finished two days before Task A (or may be started two days after Task A begins). It makes no difference if something can be done to shorten Task B; the overall schedule won't be affected. The only way to compress the overall schedule is to shorten Task A, so this is the task to be expedited. Task A is known as the critical path. A day saved on Task A will be a day saved on the entire project.

Extend this logic to thousands of tasks with thousands of dependencies and the value of the process becomes apparent. If the tasks on the critical path can be identified and expedited, the entire schedule can be compressed. This is virtually impossible to do in a meaningful way manually; a computer is required. Critical path schedules, sometimes called PERT charts after the U. S. Navy project where the concept was developed to expedite the construction of nuclear submarines, are used extensively on large construction projects; less so by architects and interior designers or for smaller projects. It demands a great deal of time to implement, but for some applications it can be worth the effort.

Scheduling Problems

Key to the scheduling activity is the determination of the duration of a given task. Once a task is defined, the man-hours required to perform that task are relatively fixed and can be accurately predicted by an experienced architect, interior designer, or contractor. Little can be done to change these hours. There are options, however. Adding more people to a task can sometimes reduce its duration. This solution has limits. Just because one person requires eight hours to do a task does not mean that the same task may be completed by eight people in one hour. The learning curve and logistical problems often severely limit adding "warm bodies" as a solution to schedule problems.

Replacing less experienced staff with more senior people may be a solution to scheduling problems. In most cases an experienced professional can produce much more in significantly less time.

Another solution is to increase an individual's working hours within a given time period—working overtime. This, too, has its limits. Effectiveness diminishes severely if the overtime is extended. The charette—the 'round the clock work done by the design team immediately before a deadline—may be inevitable and necessary but is seldom efficient in terms of productivity. A better solution to a potential schedule problem is weekend work or the addition of a few extra hours to each working day over an extended period.

CHAPTER SEVEN

DESIGN

After the program is approved, design begins. In a typical professional services contract, design includes two phases: schematic design and design development. *Schematic design*, primarily space planning, is two-dimensional. *Design development* is the expansion of the space plan into three dimensions.

Good design is more than a literal translation of a program. The formal project program provides the operational requirements for the space planning and design development of an office project. It prescribes the number of people, what they do, and how the office should function. Design, however, is not generated by people counts and functional requirements alone.

In the first century B.C., the Roman architect Vitruvius defined the qualities of good design as "commodity, firmness, and delight" (sometimes translated as "convenience, durability, and beauty"). With respect to office design, *commodity* refers to meeting the functional needs of the project, *firmness*, to the quality of construction and furnishing, and *delight*, to the aesthetic values that contribute to the quality of life of the client.

Successful design is realized when the architect or interior designer addresses these fundamental issues to generate a concept—a set of consistent ideas that define the design solution. This is what separates architecture from mere building; design from the simple satisfaction of program. Central to this process is the inspiration that comes to an architect or interior designer prepared by education and experience and a thorough understanding of the real needs of the client.

Design is the result of thousands of decisions, large and small, on everything from the location of a room to the color of a door. A design concept is the idea that integrates these decisions with clarity, character, and aesthetic logic. A successful design concept is functionally efficient, psychologically satisfying, and uplifting to the spirit.

Solving the problems of the office is not strictly, nor perhaps even primarily, the responsibility of architects or interior designers. Good environmental design is certainly part of the solution, but innovation is required from industrial designers in the production of furnishings and materials; from scientists and engineers in the development of the tools of the office, such as computers; and from management in the improvement of operational systems and personnel policies.

Good design has a timeless quality. It exhibits a simplicity of concept and a clarity of intention. There is a consistency of thought, easily traced, that runs through all elements of the project. It elicits an "Aha! Why didn't I think of that?" response. There is a sense of inevitability as if, given the program, it is the only logical solution.

Good design is the result of conscious choice. For every valid design concept there exists an equally valid but opposite concept. There is Gothic versus classical, dynamic versus static, colorful versus monochromatic, and geometric versus free form. Each of these ideas may contribute to a valid solution; the designer's choice between conflicting ideas determines the quality of the result.

Good design is not automatic. It requires time and thought. The variables to be considered are infinite, and the quick or clever solution is seldom best in the long run.

Knowledge of history and theory is indispensable to the architect or interior designer. Through study, one learns what works and what doesn't, what problems have been solved and how, and how to analyze a problem and develop a solution.

Good design almost always requires a good client. The client must have the patience to allow the designer the time to develop the solution, the intelligence and understanding to positively critique the result, and the enthusiasm to encourage the architect or interior designer to do his or her best.

While striving for objective quality, good design is essentially a subjective, individual act. Design by committee usually doesn't work. This is not to say that many people cannot contribute to the process, only that the conceptual essence of a project is almost always the product of a single mind.

The specific working methodology used by different architects and interior designers in the development of a design concept varies widely. Some visualize solutions as three-dimensional wholes, others build their solutions from considerations of mathematical modularity, and still others begin with sketches of circulation paths and functional relationships.

A space program answers only some of the questions that must be asked in the creation of an office design. Equally important are fundamental questions regarding the relationship between design and the nature of office work. These include issues of productivity and wellbeing, communication, flexibility, privacy, image and corporate culture, energy conservation and ecology, and economy.

Productivity and Wellbeing

The purpose of an office is to provide an environment in which people perform certain operations in the furtherance of the client's business. How well they perform these operations—how productive they are—depends to some extent on their wellbeing. In Charles Dickens' *A Christmas Carol*, the clerk, Bob Cratchit, is restricted to a single lump of coal and so sits bundled against the cold working on his accounts with frozen fingers. Mr. Scrooge saw no connection between human comfort and productivity.

This connection been well established. It was addressed in a study conducted by Michael Brill and his associates at the Buffalo Organization for Social and Technological Innovation (BOSTI), published in 1985. They found objective, statistical data relating office space, enclosure, layout, flexibility, privacy, and appearance, to the bottom line measures of environmental satisfaction, ease of communication, job satisfaction, and job performance.

Wellbeing and quality of life take many forms. A comfortable chair, convenient worksurface, adequate air conditioning, proper lighting, a sense of privacy, noise control, a properly designed computer keyboard and screen, and the availability of rest rooms, coffee stations, and other amenities all affect human comfort, which in turn affects employee health, morale, and productivity.

Interpersonal Communication

The facilitation of verbal communication might well be the most important single purpose of the office. Meetings in the workplace, in conference rooms, and at the coffee machine and water cooler constitute the primary means of human communication in the office. The office exists so that this can happen. The responsibility of the architect or interior designer is to enhance the process.

The layout and design of the office can help or hinder communication. Communication can be welcome and positive, contributing to the goals of the organization, or it can be unwelcome and disturbing, compromising privacy. Those located in major circulation paths or too close to the water cooler may find it difficult to concentrate. Conversely, those in isolated locations may miss the involvement with fellow workers. If the circulation path to those with whom one must communicate is too long or too circuitous, communication will be discouraged.

Flexibility

Basically a management issue, an approach to flexibility is a decision that must be made early in the design process. Flexibility refers to the ability to reorganize office space in response to

functional change. Flexibility costs money and may require sacrifices in other areas. It may not be a requirement in all projects. Although some companies claim that they move or change 30 percent of their open plan workstations every year, a law office may remain unchanged throughout the life of a ten- or twenty-year lease.

Flexibility in office space may be obtained in a variety of ways. One approach is to maximize the standardization of offices and open plan workstations. Under this scenario organizational change is accomplished by moving personnel with minimal reconstruction and furniture reconfiguration. An extreme example of this approach is the *free address* concept, where employees are not assigned their own dedicated workstation but may select any one that is unoccupied. Once they log on to the computer and telecommunications system, they are ready to work.

An opposite strategy takes full advantage of the modularity and ease of reconfiguration of demountable partitions and open plan workstation systems. Each organizational change results in a new space arrangement and workstation layout. Strict adherence to modularity can minimize changes to ceilings, light fixtures, and wiring distribution.

An example of a modular approach to space planning is the concept of *universal planning* explored by Christine Banks of Gensler and Associates. Under this concept, the office circulation path is fixed and the allowable areas for open plan workstations predetermined. Workstations for different staff levels are then selected with common and related footprint dimensions, such as 8' by 6', 8' by 8', and 8' by 12'. As a result, a designated floor space 16' by 24', for example, can accommodate four 12' workstations, six

8' workstations, eight 6' workstations, or various combinations of the three sizes, which can be mixed and matched and changed while still maintaining the overall design concept.

Privacy

Privacy is another management issue. A decision must be made concerning which employees will occupy private offices, which will occupy shared offices, and which will be located in open workstations. Sometimes this is mandated in the programming phase; sometimes this is the result of studies of alternate design approaches prepared by the architect or interior designer during space planning.

The assignment of private offices is often a matter of status and tradition. In many organizations the private office is a symbol of success. It indicates that its occupant has achieved a position superior to that of other employees. The location, size, and design of the private office tells much about an organization's management style and corporate culture.

A major advantage of the private office is acoustical privacy. In many fields, the need to talk without being overheard is paramount. The legal profession is particularly sensitive to this, citing the obligation to preserve client confidentiality. Personnel managers and others who deal with employee problems may also have a strong desire for acoustical privacy. A major complaint of workers in open plan workstations is often the lack of this privacy.

On the other hand, retail banks have a tradition of open planning with little or no privacy. In a typical platform area, officers sit at open desks ready to greet customers with an image of friendliness and honesty. As a consequence, bankers will tolerate an openness in office planning that most lawyers would find unacceptable.

The concept of the closed private office as status symbol was challenged in the headquarters for the Weyerhauser Corporation in Tacoma, Washington, designed by Skidmore, Owings and Merrill in 1971. In this project there were no private offices. Everyone, including the president, occupied an open workstation. This project was enormously influential in introducing new ways to think about privacy.

For some, a private office can mean peace and quiet. It presents the opportunity to be alone to concentrate on one's work without distraction. Academics and researchers generally list this as an important requirement of their workplaces.

An aspect of the individual workplace related to privacy is personalization. Individual workers tend to have strong nesting instincts, a desire to make the workplace their own. Personalization and control can extend to the selection of colors and materials, furniture and components, the display of artifacts, and even lighting, acoustics, and climate control. There is a line, however, where individuality conflicts with order. Cross over that line, and the result is chaos. The determination of that line is an important decision in the design process.

Image and Corporate Culture

The office is a reflection of corporate culture. That culture is communicated to employees, customers, and the community at large through design. That designed image can be one of opulence, conservatism, progressive thinking, or many other things. The image may involve historical, cultural, national, regional, and ethnic values. The design of the office can help to reinforce the image, change the image, or, conversely, repudiate the image.

Quality design can influence customers, and many companies embellish their public contact spaces at the expense of operational areas. This may improve sales; it may also send a negative message to the back office workforce.

A positive image can help in the recruitment and retention of quality staff. Well-designed offices can instill pride in an organization. The provision of amenities may be important in this respect. Food service and lounge areas, health and physical fitness facilities, and day care centers provide opportunities for a change in atmosphere, and they can function as accents to the overall design concept.

Energy Conservation and Ecology

Prior to the energy crisis of 1973 little thought was given to energy conservation. The cost of power was relatively low. When oil supplies diminished and prices rose dramatically, energy conservation began to emerge as an economic and ecological necessity. Energy limits were imposed, and landlords, architects, engineers, and interior designers all sought ways to significantly reduce energy usage.

There are other ecological concerns. The use of certain woods popular in office construction may contribute to the destruction of the rain forests. Other materials, such as plastics, may pose ecological hazards in their fabrication and ultimate disposal.

Economy

Successful design is almost always a response to constraints. Projects without boundaries seldom seem to generate the quality of those where limitations are well defined. Constraints force the architect and interior designer to set priorities, to examine alternatives, and to make choices. Nothing is arbitrary; everything is the result of thorough understanding and analysis. This process inevitably results in a superior product.

One of the most powerful constraints on any project is the budget. Rather than restricting the design process, budget limitations can give focus to the development of design concepts.

SCHEMATIC DESIGN

Space plans begin with an accurate drawing of the base building floor plan. Existing building drawings are usually available from the base building architects through the building owner. For older buildings, municipal building departments may be a good source for documents. If all else fails, measured drawings may have to be done. Documents of the existing space should be as complete as possible and should include engineering drawings and records of any previous tenant construction work. Eventually all this information will be needed. Although the architect or interior designer may perform the legwork required to obtain the documents, the client is usually contractually responsible for providing these drawings, and, unless otherwise agreed, the design firm may rely on these documents in doing its work and cannot be held liable for any errors they may contain.

The architect or interior designer should redraw the background as accurately and completely as possible. Actual dimensions should be used; scaling prints is very dangerous and should be avoided whenever possible. Not only does paper shrink and stretch, but dimensions are often changed during construction without the drawing being revised.

Base building backgrounds will be used many times before the project is complete. If not computerized, the backgrounds should be drawn on a substantial medium such as ink on mylar. On this background the architect or interior designer prepares the space plan showing proposed locations of partitions, doors, cabinetwork, and furnishings. Early in the process the drawings may be somewhat sketchy; however, final space plans are usually carefully drafted, sometimes with rendering and materials delineation. A space plan must be convincing to the client and should be attractive and professionally presented.

Space plans are usually drawn to a scale of 1/8" = 1'0". For small projects 1/4" = 1'0" may be used and for very large projects, 1/16" = 1'0". Unusual scales should be avoided, even though they may sometimes have advantages, such as fitting a particular drawing sheet size. A drawing scale is a matter of perception, as people become accustomed to seeing things at a certain size. A drawing at a scale of 3/32" = 1'0", for example,

may be perceived by the eye as being at 1/8" scale and may look too crowded or be otherwise misunderstood. The same principle applies when having drawings photographically reduced or enlarged.

The purpose of schematic design is to provide a layout that responds to the program, as well as to issues of productivity and wellbeing. Some of the design principles or tools used to accomplish this are the spatial arrangement of solids and voids, modularity, and patterns of circulation.

Space

Although drawn in two dimensions, a space plan is conceptualized in the mind of the architect or interior designer as an arrangement of three-dimensional volumes in space. Space is the defining characteristic of architecture. More than structure, surface, or ornamentation, what one feels most strongly in a Gothic cathedral or Roman temple is the shape

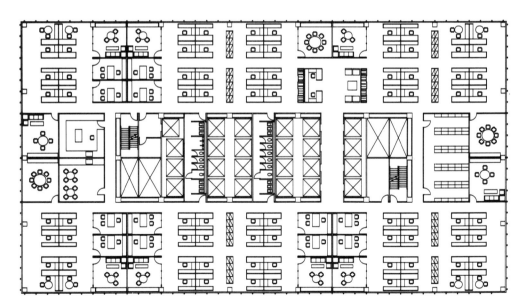

SPACE PLAN.

and character of the interior volume. Space is the empty void defined by surrounding solids—walls, columns, ceiling, and floor.

In the design of the office, the solids are the building core and other closed rooms, and the voids are the corridors and open work areas. Manipulation of these spatial solids and voids is a basic conceptual tool. Hidden away in the space program is a pattern of solids and voids in different sizes and in different proportions; a rhythm of repetitions of elements and perhaps symmetry; a regular arrangement of spaces creating a sense of order. Like a sculptor discovering the figure inside a block of marble, space planning for some is the search to discover the pattern implicit in the program.

Variety in the size of spaces can provide interest. Spaces whose boundaries are well defined can provide security and a sense of place. Spaces that are ill defined and randomly arranged can cause confusion. Spaces that are too large make workers feel lost in a "sea of desks."

Spatial interest may be enhanced by views to the exterior. Outside views provide psychological relief and physical rest for the eyes. These values are considered so important that some European countries legally mandate that all office workers be within sight of an exterior window.

Modularity

One guide for establishing the aesthetic pattern of solids and voids in a space plan is the modularity of base building elements, construction materials, and furnishings. At the largest scale is the pattern of building column bays. These may be subdivided by a regular arrangement of window mullions. Ceiling tiles, light fixtures, and furniture systems are inherently modular interior components that can bring order to a design concept.

Modularity has a practical aspect. The interchangeability implicit in modular design may increase flexibility both in terms of layout and in the reuse of materials and furnishings.

Circulation

The circulation path defines the skeletal framework of the office. Whether an enclosed corridor or a pathway through an open work area, a circulation path is meant to get people easily from place to place. It also arranges and connects spaces into regular patterns. Through the fourth dimension of time, the memory organizes these patterns into a coherent whole.

A successful circulation path gives a person a sense of both where they are in the overall plan of the office and where they are going by providing information and landmarks along the way. A circulation path need not be strictly rectilinear but should conform to a comprehensible concept. Large office suites can be disorienting, particularly ones with many rooms and enclosed corridors. A poor circulation path can make a person feel claustrophobic or literally lost.

DESIGN DEVELOPMENT

After approval of schematic design, the three-dimensional realization of the space plan takes place during design development. Elevations, perspectives, and/or isometric drawings are produced, study models built, and material samples collected. Elements not shown in a space plan, such as ceiling conditions and lighting, are studied. Engineering concepts are developed. Furnishings are researched and selected. Modifications to the space plan inevitably occur as the design is refined. The end result of the design development phase should be complete documentation of the design intent from which construction drawings and specifications can be prepared.

Proportion and scale, color and texture, and the quality of light are the tools of design development. The context, or building within which the office is situated, must be respected.

Base Building Influences

The building within which an office space is constructed can influence the project design. Details and materials used on the exterior window wall, the core and elevator cabs, as well as the overall concept of the structure itself may not necessarily be directly copied, but they must be respected, and an appropriate relationship with the office design concept must be developed.

The flat acoustical tile ceiling of the modern office building may limit spatial manipulation to the horizontal plane. Despite physical interference of structure and mechanical ductwork, architects and interior designers often go to great lengths to raise or lower ceilings to give a vertical component to spatial definition. This accounts for the popularity of older industrial and loft buildings for conversion to office use. High, irregular ceilings, with interesting structural patterns, add a third dimension to spatial expression.

Scale and Proportion

Scale and proportion control all elements of the office interior. They affect the size of rooms, the detailing of wood paneling, and the selection of accessories. Well-proportioned materials and systems and appropriate relationships between them can create a sense of comfort and aesthetic satisfaction. When poorly conceived, scale and proportion can lead to boredom or confusion.

A module is a unit of measure used for regulating proportions. In ancient Greece proportion was a result of geometry; the "golden rectangle" was one manifestation. Greek architecture and the Greek orders were based on elegant but complex rules of proportion. In this century the Swiss architect Le Corbusier developed a system based on ideal human dimensions called the *Modulor*, or "golden module," which served as the basis for all of the proportions and dimensions in his buildings.

Color, Texture, and Lighting

Color and texture are inherent characteristics of building materials and furnishings. Much has been written about the psychological effects of color—red is exciting, yellow is cheerful, green is restful, and so forth. Probably more important than the color hue itself, however, are its value, intensity, and contrast with other colors in the space. In retail shops and restaurants, color may be used forcefully, deliberately intended to catch the eye. In office work areas, however, strong colors may be a distraction and a subtle color scheme may be more appropriate. In office projects, striking effects may need to be limited to reception rooms, food service areas, or lounges.

Texture adds tactile values and can provide visual interest through modulation of light and shadow. A textured surface enhances sound absorbency by increasing surface area.

Color and texture exist not as isolated elements but in relationships that create an integrated and harmonious whole. Whether smooth or rough, monochromatic or high contrast, the use of color and texture should exhibit a consistency of design intent.

Color and texture are affected by the direction, quality, and intensity of light. In some areas dramatic accent lighting may be used to highlight design elements. In general office areas the problems are of a different sort. The level of ambient light, provision of task lighting for reference material, and the avoidance of glare are practical design problems to be solved.

Materials

Integrity in the selection and use of materials has been of major philosophical and aesthetic interest to architects and interior designers for most of this century. On one side are those, such as Frank Lloyd Wright, who feel that each material has a unique nature and that its use must be true to that character. Another school of thought sees validity in faux materials. Trompe l'oeil has a long history in interior decoration, and the painting of plaster columns to look like marble, for example, is a tradition that postmodernist theory has once again made acceptable.

Care should be used with faux materials. It may be acceptable to fool the eye, but one should not try to fool the mind. Faux materials used as the result of a deliberate design concept is one thing; used to cheaply imitate a better material is something else entirely.

Appearance is not the only attribute of a material that should be considered. Ludwig Mies van der Rohe said "God is in the details." He believed that there were right and wrong ways to select materials and put them together. There is an innate integrity to careful and appropriate selection and detailing that gives intellectual and aesthetic strength to a project.

DESIGN PRESENTATION

Periodically during the design process the architect or interior designer must meet with the client to review and seek approval of the design. Design presentations are made at different times, to different groups, and for different purposes. The executive committee, for example, may be interested in overall concepts and image, the facility management group may want to review budgets and schedules, while the user groups will want to approve functional layouts. The when, where, who, what, and why of each presentation should be clearly understood and stated in the agenda.

There should be no surprises at design presentations. Numerous limited reviews at each step along the way are generally more successful then one big presentation. Presentations are successful when what is being shown is a logical, easily understood progression from the previous presentation. If the client is unprepared by what is presented, the credibility of the architect or interior designer as well as weeks or months of time may be jeopardized.

The client representative on the design team can be a major factor in orchestrating a successful presentation. If he or she is fully integrated into the design process and has reviewed and approved the presentation ahead of time, a subtle transformation of responsibility takes place. The "we/they" relationship is replaced with an "us," and the client representative may become the strongest defender of the solution being presented.

Like marketing presentations, design presentations require skill and practice. Presentations should be organized, outlined, and rehearsed. A comfortable location should be selected with drawings and samples arranged ahead of time. An agenda should be prepared with the issues to be resolved clearly stated. When many drawings or presentation boards are to be shown, they should be organized on the wall in the order in which they will be discussed. Some architects and interior designers prefer stacking drawings on an easel with only one drawing visible at a time. They feel this progressive disclosure concentrates the attention of the audience and minimizes distractions.

When presenting space plans, it is usually a good idea to begin with an orientation to the base building, then to walk the client through the space beginning with the elevator lobby or entry to the office space.

Alternate plans, details, or selections of materials or furnishings should be presented on separate drawings or boards. Once an alternate has been rejected, it should immediately be removed from view so as not to detract from the balance of the presentation.

Presentations are often made several times to different audiences with different information given to each. Titles or other graphic devices that force drawings to be arranged in a particular order should be avoided. Each drawing should have a title and date and be able to stand alone.

Clients often have difficulty understanding drawings. Space plans for presentation to clients should look attractive and as "real" as possible. Furniture gives a sense of scale and realism to a drawing. Shadows, when drawn below and to one side of a piece of furniture, give a three-dimensional effect. A bird's-eye isometric drawing is more time consuming to produce but may increase the client's understanding.

Models can be effective presentation tools. These need not always be professionally prepared; often study models of small areas are helpful.

If the project is being produced on a computer-aided design and drafting (CADD) system, even the initial space plan presentation may include a computer-generated perspective. Some firms present projects to their clients on the computer screen or use videotape to walk through the project with a series of continually changing eye-level perspectives.

As a general rule, all drawings presented to clients should be reproducible. Copies will be required for marking changes, for the client's records, for the design firm's records and perhaps for engineers and the landlord. Ink on illustration board or elaborately colored prints that cannot be reproduced are usually to be avoided.

In accordance with most professional service contracts, drawings must be formally approved by clients at certain times during the project. These are benchmarks that allow the project to proceed to the next phase. On large projects the approval process may be complex, with supervisors, department heads, facility managers, and others at various levels in the organization, each having the right of review. This can take weeks or months with approvals phased by planning unit or department. To maintain order, many firms draft an approval block directly on the space plan or make a rubber stamp for prints that contains blanks for signatures and dates of each person who reviews and approves the document. Approvals shown directly on drawings provide a clear, unambiguous record.

CONSULTANTS

The specialized consultants that will be needed on a project generally begin work during the design phases of the project. At a minimum, the services of mechanical and electrical engineers are required on almost every project. Depending on project size and complexity, many other consultants may be needed. These may include a graphics designer, structural engineer, and consultants specializing in lighting, telecommunications, audio-visual, acoustics, artwork, and records management.

Mechanical Engineer

Mechanical engineers are responsible for the design and documentation of the heating, ventilating, and air conditioning (HVAC) system. This includes the extension of the base building mechanical system into the office space, system modification to handle special conditions, and the specification of supplemental systems where required. They generally also perform fire protection (sprinkler) and plumbing design. In plumbing design, the architect or interior designer selects the visible fixtures, and the engineer designs the piping.

Electrical Engineer

Electrical engineers are responsible for the design and documentation of electrical power and lighting. They assist the architect or interior designer in the selection and location of outlets and light fixtures and provide the documentation of the circuiting and panel requirements.

Lighting Consultant

Decorative lighting, accent lighting for artwork, and lighting to accommodate audio-visual facilities may require the services of a lighting consultant. On very large projects they may assist in the design, calculation, and testing of general office lighting. Lighting consultants may practice independently or be associated with electrical engineers.

Structural Engineer

If the furnishings or equipment to be installed in the space are extraordinarily heavy or if stairs between floors are being considered, the services of a structural engineer will be required. Some landlords insist that all tenant designs be reviewed and approved, for a fee, by the building's structural engineer. Structural engineers check whether heavy equipment, files, or storage cabinets will require structural reinforcement, and then they design and document that work. They identify allowable locations for floor openings and provide design and documentation for new tenant interconnecting stairs. Structural engineering work is usually minimal on most office interior projects. In old, structurally questionable buildings, however, this work can be extensive.

Audio-visual Consultant

Audio-visual consultants design and document microphone and loudspeaker systems, recording systems, projection systems, and video systems including video teleconferencing. Their work may be found in conference and board rooms, classrooms, and auditoriums.

Acoustical Consultant

Acoustical consultants review the plans and details prepared by the architect or interior designer and advise concerning anticipated sound levels and acoustical problems. The acoustical consultant may test specific areas, supervise acoustical mock-ups, or recommend remedial action. An acoustical consultant can provide a high level of psychological comfort at relatively low cost to such clients as attorneys or others with particular concerns about acoustics and confidentiality of speech.

Food Service Consultant

If the new office project contains a cafeteria, executive dining room, or other major food service facility, a food service consultant will usually be required. Food service consultants provide advice about the size and type of corporate eating facilities and prepare detailed designs. and construction drawings and specifications for commercial kitchens.

Artwork Consultant

Working closely with the design firm, an artwork consultant may advise concerning the selection and placement of paintings, sculpture, and other artwork in the new offices. For corporations with large and valuable collections, this work can be extensive.

Records Management Consultant

A records management consultant specializes in filing systems, particularly with regard to document standardization, retention, disposal, and dead filing.

This work is not necessarily directly related to new construction, but a new office project provides an ideal opportunity to conduct such a study.

Graphic Designer

At a minimum, graphics consultants prepare signage for office space, including firm identification, directional, and identification signage. In a larger context, graphics consultants may provide full corporate identity programs, which include the development of distinctive graphic imagery for the organization and its implementation in everything from stationery, annual reports, business forms, and advertising to environmental signage.

CHAPTER EIGHT

CODES AND STANDARDS

Interior planning and design is not done in a vacuum. There are many rules and restrictions that must be fully understood and complied with. Building codes, requirements for access and use by the disabled, asbestos concerns, and many other regulations affect office projects and have significant implications for design. It is advisable to perform an organized check for applicable regulations in the jurisdiction where the project is located. This should be done early in the project, not delayed until the construction document phase.

Codes and standards generally represent minimum acceptable criteria; they are not formulas for good design.

Interior office construction, like all construction, is regulated by the requirements of local building codes. Most large cities have written their own detailed building codes; many smaller jurisdictions have adopted one of the standard national codes, such as the Uniform Building Code (UBC), Basic Building Code of the Building Officials and Code Administrators International (BOCA), or the Standard Building Code of the Southern Building Code Congress. These regulations are enforced when plans are checked during the application process for a building permit and by building inspectors who make job site inspections. A final inspection may be made just prior to moving in order to obtain an occupancy permit.

Building codes are subject to constant change and revision; architects and interior designers must always be sure they are using the latest version.

Codes often refer to standards developed by the federal government or private organizations. Among the best known are the American Standard for Testing and Materials (ASTM), American National Standards Institute (ANSI), Factory Mutual, and Underwriters Laboratories (UL). ASTM and ANSI, along with the federal government, are known for their specification standards for almost all materials used in construction. Factory Mutual and UL maintain testing laboratories that determine the flammability and other characteristics of wall finishes, electrical devices, and other materials and construction systems.

For electrical work, the National Electrical Code is almost universally recognized.

In addition to building departments, municipal fire departments often take an interest in construction progress, enforcing their own regulations and performing their own inspections. They commonly enforce the Life Safety Code of the National Fire Protection Association (NFPA).

A major concern addressed by all of these regulations is fire safety. One aspect of fire safety is preventing the spread of fire from one part of a building to another. Local building codes define the precise requirements for fire protection for the components of all classes of buildings. The requirements for high-rise buildings are much more stringent than those for low-rise buildings primarily because of the difficulty fire fighters have in reaching a fire site.

The ability of a partition or other barrier to control fire is stated as the number of hours of exposure to fire that is required before failure. For example, the structural frame of a high-rise office building may be required by the building code to have a four-hour rating, while the partitions surrounding the exit stairs may be required to have a two-hour rating.

Interior office partitions are generally either unrated for normal interior construction, one-hour rated for horizontal exitway protection, and two-hour rated for protection of vertical openings and stairs. Rated partitions must be continuous from the floor to the underside of the floor slab above, and all openings for doors or ductwork must be similarly rated.

Interior office partitions and doors can protect occupants by providing areas of refuge and protected passageways to fire stairs and exits. Floors may be subdivided into safe *compartments* by partitions with one- and two-hour ratings. Current New York City laws, for example, require that office floors in unsprinklered buildings be divided by two-hour partitions into areas not to exceed 15,000 square feet and further subdivided by one-hour partitions into areas not to exceed 7,500 square feet.

Building codes regulate the use of potentially dangerous finish materials by defining *flame spread ratings*. A flame spread rating or index is a numerical value for the flammability characteristics of applied surface finish materials compared to untreated red oak, which is arbitrarily assigned a rating of 100. Codes then restrict the allowable flame spread ratings in spaces according to space use. Finishes in fire stairs may be restricted to materials with a flame spread rating of under 25, for example, while other finishes in office space may require ratings of 75 or less. Particular attention should be paid to adhesives and backing materials. Finishes less than 1/28" thick may be exempt as may doors and trim that cover less than 10 percent of the wall surface.

In the enforcement of flame spread regulations, municipal building departments typically require certification from a recognized testing laboratory, such as Underwriters Laboratories. If this certification is not provided by the finish manufacturer, a new test may have to be performed. This can be expensive and time consuming. For this reason, exotic or foreign finish materials may not be feasible for a particular project.

Municipal building departments are not the only enforcement agencies regulating construction. There are also federal regulators such as the Occupational Safety and Health Administration (OSHA). In many locations labor unions can have a significant effect on office construction and furnishing. They may be in a position to dictate which workers are allowed on the project site, the allocation of work between trades, acceptable products and approved methods of installation.

Building codes are formidable documents. Fortunately, relatively few chapters apply to the development of interior office space.

Although all building codes follow the same general principals in protecting the health and safety of the public, there is considerable variation between localities in detailed requirements. The following list is a guide to the kinds of regulations typically included in building codes. This is the information that should be investigated during a code check.

❏ Determination of occupancy classification and building construction type based on fire resistance. Construction requirements for fire protection including shaft enclosures and stairway construction.

❏ Determination of the occupant load factor in terms of square feet per person and total occupant load. Determination of the number of exits required, access to exits, distance to and between exits, minimum width of exits and exit passageways, and dead-end corridor limitations.

❏ Requirements for automatic sprinkler systems and bonuses allowed for buildings so equipped.

❏ Ceiling construction requirements including earthquake bracing. Minimum ceiling height requirements.

❏ Requirements for partition construction including the use of fire-retardant wood. Requirements for fire-rated construction and fire containment or compartmentation requirements.

❏ Requirements for the width, height, fire rating, door swing, and identification of exit doors and doors in fire-rated partitions. Requirements for hardware including locks and closing devices.

❏ Structural floor-loading limitations and requirements for floor reinforcement.

❏ Construction requirements for fire stairs and interior convenience stairs including riser/tread proportions and dimension limitations. Requirements concerning the allowable height between landings, stair widths, headroom, railing heights, landing sizes, and the protection of openings between floors. Restrictions on the use of circular and spiral stairs.

❏ Construction requirements for ramps including maximum allowable slope and railing heights and locations.

❏ Life safety requirements for smoke control, exit signs, emergency communications, smoke detection, annunciating and alarm systems, exit location diagrams, exit illumination, fire alarm pull boxes, fire extinguishers, and emergency power. Regulations concerning the use of fire suppression systems such as Halon. Restrictions on elevator usage during fire emergencies.

❏ Requirements for the protection of electrical and communications wiring including the use of conduit for electrical wiring. Allowable coatings for unenclosed communication and low voltage wiring. Restrictions on the use of plastics that emit toxic fumes when burning.

❏ Plumbing fixture requirements based on occupant load.

❏ Requirements for glazing, including

area limitations, glazing support, and the use of tempered and laminated safety glass. Glass railing requirements.

❑ Atrium and mezzanine requirements. Requirements for special facilities for places of assembly, food service, vertical conveyors, and escalators.

❑ Interior finish flame spread classifications. Requirements for wall coverings, draperies, and carpeting including adhesives and backing materials. Flame spread requirements based on room use. Exceptions for trim and exceptions based on the percentage of wall covered and thickness of finish material.

❑ Energy regulations including maximum allowable watts per square foot. Light switching requirements.

ACCESSIBILITY FOR THE DISABLED

As a general principle the opportunity to work in an office cannot be denied a person because of physical disabilities. In addition to state and local laws regarding accessibility, federal regulations, especially the Americans with Disabilities Act (ADA) of 1990, now require equal opportunity for people with disabilities. This means that, within reason, nothing in the office should be designed to prevent full use by the disabled.

Regulations regarding workplace access and use by the disabled may vary depending on locality. Compliance requirements may differ depending on the number of employees in the new offices and the extent of construction work in the project. Exact detailed requirements are complex, and there are often several options available to achieve the same end. As part of a code check, architects and interior designers need to be aware of applicable provisions of these laws. Following are some of the requirements that should be examined for their effect on the design of office space:

❑ Minimum widths for corridors, passageways, and doors to allow passage by wheelchairs. Requirements for adequate clearance for turning corners and making U-turns.

❑ Restrictions on floor-level changes including the provision of ramps for wheelchair access. Requirements for ramp slopes, landings, and width.

❑ Height and clear lap space requirements for desks, kitchen counters, work counters, sinks, and drinking fountains to allow use while seated in a wheelchair.

❑ Use of levers rather than knobs for door handles and faucets.

❑ Maximum allowable reach dimensions for towels, dispensers, and shelves.

❑ Requirements for wide stalls and grab bars in toilet facilities. Requirements for specially designed sinks, water closets, and other plumbing fixtures. Adequate floor space requirements for wheelchair maneuvering.

❑ Minimum heights for electrical wall outlets for accessibility from a wheelchair.

❑ Requirements for raised letters and symbols and provisions of audible signals and warnings for the visually impaired.

❑ Visual signals and alarms for the hearing impaired. Provision of telephones for the hearing and speech impaired.

[handwritten margin notes:] LANDING AS WIDE AS WIDEST POINT OF RAMP × 60" LONG

IF A CHANGE OF DIRECTION A LANDING 60" × 60"

GRAB BARS 33"-36" H

36" MIN CLEAR WIDTH

HANDRAIL NEEDED IF RISE IS MORE THAN 6"

RAMP SLOPE 1:12, IF MORE THAN 30" RISE NEED TO BE A "REST"

❏ Limitations on carpet firmness, pile height, and total height.

❏ Restriction of open stair treads and requirements for sloped stair riser faces.

❏ Requirements for the insulation of pipes and other hot surfaces.

FURNISHINGS STANDARDS

Interior movable furnishings are generally not covered by building codes although they can present a significant hazard in the case of fire. Voluntary standards for evaluating the safety, durability, and structural adequacy of movable furnishings, including the flammability of upholstered furniture, are developed by the Business and Institutional Furniture Manufacturers Association (BIFMA). These standards define specific test methodology and minimum acceptance levels.

ASBESTOS AND OTHER ENVIRONMENTAL CONCERNS

Breathing asbestos fibers in the air has been shown to cause cancer and other lung problems. Before its dangers were recognized, massive amounts of asbestos were used in buildings as fireproofing. Since the early 1970s many regulations by OSHA, the Environmental Protection Agency (EPA) and other governmental bodies on the federal, state, and local levels have been enacted to protect workers from the dangers posed by asbestos fibers.

Generally, there are three possible solutions to asbestos problems. The first is leaving it alone; undisturbed asbestos may not become airborne and may therefore not pose a health risk. The second is encapsulation, surrounding the asbestos with a permanent impregnable shield. The third is removal, which is ultimately

the safest but can cause serious problems during implementation.

Analyzing and treating asbestos problems in buildings is a specialized field with high liability risks for its practitioners. If the presence of asbestos is suspected, a specialist should be consulted. Architects and interior designers should check with their attorneys and liability insurance carriers before offering advice or recommendations regarding asbestos.

Indoor Air Quality

The modern office building is sealed tight against the outside environment. Windows typically don't open and air movement is mechanically controlled by the HVAC system. To comply with energy conservation requirements the circulation of fresh air through office space is often restricted. This can pose chemical and bacteriological situations that may, over the long term, seriously affect employee health. These are usually grouped together and known as *sick building syndrome.*

Causes include chemical vapors from office copiers and other equipment, formaldehyde and other vapors from adhesives used in construction and carpeting, tobacco smoke, and fungus and bacteria growth in HVAC ductwork or damp areas. Increasing air circulation almost always improves the situation, but care should also be taken in the specification of safe products and in the cleaning and maintenance of the offices.

Computer Terminal Problems

Unlike typewriters and other office equipment of the past, computer terminals have no manual carriage returns and no paper to change, nothing in fact to take the hands away from the keyboard to provide variety in movement. This can cause serious musculo-skeletal disorders to the hands, wrists, arms, shoulders, and lower back. Improper lighting can cause eye strain and eye fatigue, and there is some concern about the effects of radiation. Many jurisdictions now have regulations affecting computer terminal use. Design regulations may include glare shielding, ergonomic furnishings, and changes in equipment design. Management solutions may involve training in the use of equipment to avoid health problems and mandatory rest periods and other relief from continuous keyboard use.

CHAPTER NINE

CONSTRUCTION
MATERIALS
AND SYSTEMS

A major achievement of American ingenuity and invention is the high-rise office building, which was developed in the late nineteenth century. More than any other building type, this structure defines the heart of our cities. For the skyscraper to reach its full potential for its users, however, another remarkable achievement was required—lightweight interior construction, which was developed in the mid-twentieth century.

Traditional architectural thinking assumes that the interior and exterior of a building are aspects of the same problem. The interior is a reflection of the exterior design; it is an extension of the same concept, done by the same designer. A building is designed to fit a specific function, such as church, house, or school, and that function, even the exact room configuration, remains fixed until the building is demolished. The great monuments of the architectural past, the Gothic cathedrals and royal palaces, appear today, inside and out, much as they did when they were built. The idea that the function and layout of the inside of these buildings would ever change was never remotely considered by their architects.

Thus it was with the early skyscrapers. Permanent corridors and rooms were arranged and built of hard plaster with marble wainscots. Occupants were expected to conform their operations to the layout, not the other way around.

Then several events happened. The first was technological: the invention of air conditioning and the dramatic increase in the amount of wiring required by electrical and telephone service. This meant that all those solid plaster ceilings and walls would have to be removed and replaced if the new machinery, ductwork, and conduit was to be accommodated. The second event occurred when initial occupants of the structures changed, grew, or moved out, so that the buildings were filled with organizations with very different space requirements. The old layouts simply didn't work for the new users.

A fundamentally new concept in architecture was emerging, one in which the exterior shell of the building and the interior configuration moved along different time lines, one measured in centuries, the other in years or a few decades at most. The interior and exterior of a building began to be viewed as relatively independent of each other. The building, in other words, was seen as a long-lived framework within which a great variety of short-lived functional activities could take place. The relatively permanent core and shell could accommodate flexible office space that could be quickly and economically reconfigured as tenants and their requirements changed.

The result is the modern office building consisting of an exterior skin, structural framework, central mechanical plant, and a core containing elevators, exit stairways, toilet rooms, and primary mechanical and electrical distribution. The office interior consists of partitions, doors, ceilings, flooring, finishes, and furnishings. Connecting the two are the secondary mechanical distribution systems and the electrical and communications wiring delivered to the occupants where needed.

PARTITIONS

Interior office partitions create rooms and define space. They are technically nonstructural, supporting nothing more than their own weight and perhaps a bookshelf or hanging wall cabinet. They may be constructed of a variety of materials, most commonly of gypsum drywall and metal studs, and may be finished with paint, wall covering, wood paneling, or other materials.

Drywall Interior Partitions

Gypsum is a gray to white mineral that, when dried and ground, forms a powdery substance called plaster of paris. When recombined with water, gypsum forms a hard, durable, fire and sound resistant material ideally suited for interior partitions and ceilings. When the recombination with water occurs at the jobsite, it is called plaster. When the recombination is done in a factory, prefabricated panels called *drywall* or gypsum wallboard are produced.

Drywall is gypsum formed into flat sheets and faced and edged with paper. Thicknesses vary from 1/4" to 1" with 5/8" being typical for interior office partitions. The standard panel width is four feet with lengths ordered as required by the ceiling height on the project. At the jobsite, the drywall panels are screwed to metal studs and the joints are covered with paper and wet plaster called spackle. The panel edges are made with a slight taper so that the addition of tape and spackle will not cause a bulge in the wall surface.

Metal studs make up the framework that holds drywall in place. The studs are made of light gauge steel, bent to a C shape, and come in a variety of widths with 2½" being the most common for interior office partitions. The metal stud framework consists of a bottom track anchored to the floor, vertical studs, and a top track anchored either to the ceiling suspension system or to the underside of the floor above. Vertical stud spacing is typically 16" on center so that each four-foot-wide drywall panel is anchored at four points across its width. Spacing at 24" on center is also common.

By themselves, drywall panels are rigid but structurally weak, while metal studs are strong but flimsy. Together they form a strong and stable composite sandwich system of great flexibility, reasonable cost, and rapid construction.

A typical standard interior partition with no special requirements for fire protection or acoustical control consists of a layer of 5/8" drywall on each side of a 2½" metal stud. Total partition thickness is 3¾". If partitions are ceiling supported, they run from the floor to the underside of the ceiling. Where required by building codes for earthquake protection, diagonal bracing may be installed from the top of the partition to the underside of the floor above.

If partitions are supported by the floor slabs, top and bottom, with the ceilings installed after the partition, the studs run from the floor to the underside of the floor slab above. The drywall on unrated partitions generally extends about 6" above the suspended ceiling.

Another form of interior partitioning is furring, which is a one-sided partition used to enclose plumbing and other shafts or to add thickness to partitions for dimensional reasons. Furring is used around columns for fire protection and to provide a finished wall surface.

Acoustical Partitions

A major function of partitions is to control sound between spaces. A measurement of the ability of materials or construction systems, such as drywall partitions, to block sound is the sound transmission class (STC) rating.

A standard interior office partition without special treatment will provide an STC rating in the range of 35 to 40. This is satisfactory for most types of office occupancy. Normal speech may be faintly heard and, with difficulty, understood.

This level of privacy, however, may not be satisfactory where confidentiality of conversations is a priority. Lawyers and personnel interviewers, for example, may demand a higher level of speech privacy. This may be accomplished by adding batt insulation in the stud space of the partition, which will increase the STC rating to between 40 to 45. If an additional layer of 5/8" gypsum wallboard is added to each side of the partition, the STC rating is increased to the range of 50 to 55.

The STC rating of a partition is affected by the meeting of the partition with other surfaces. Batt insulation and extra layers of drywall will be wasted if sound can travel around a partition at its edges or through a partition at back-to-back elec-

WHEN U ENCLOSE PIPE + SUCH

BATTING MUST ALSO BE AROUND ELECT OUTLETS

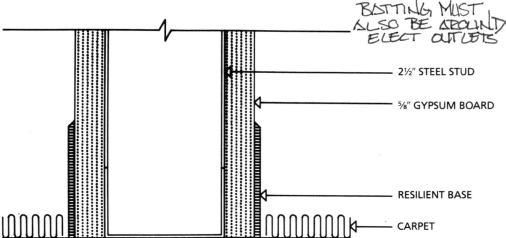

2½" STEEL STUD

⅝" GYPSUM BOARD

RESILIENT BASE

CARPET

INTERIOR PARTITION DETAIL. This is a typical detail for a standard drywall partition.

trical outlets, for example. To be acoustically effective, partitions must be continuously sealed at floor, ceiling, and adjoining partitions, including exterior building walls.

One critical edge condition occurs above the suspended ceiling. To achieve the higher STC rating, the acoustical partition may be extended through the ceiling to the underside of the floor above with care taken to provide a seal at ducts, beams, and other obstructions. To provide for the passage of air when the ceiling space is used as a return air plenum, a transfer duct, shaped like the letter Z and lined with insulation, can be used.

If the ceiling space must be kept open to facilitate air movement, another solution to controlling sound above the ceiling is to lay batt insulation above the ceiling and over the partition, extending several feet into the rooms on either side.

The connection of the interior partition to the exterior window wall of the building is often another weak link. Rubber gasketing may be used between the partition stud and metal window mullion to provide a tight seal. Curtain pockets and

heating and air conditioning units below windowsills also provide easy paths for sound into adjacent rooms. Filling such spaces with insulation often solves the problem.

Fire Rated Partitions

Another function of partitions is to control the spread of fire. Although gypsum construction is inherently fire resistive, there are special cases when these characteristics must be increased.

When fire rated construction is required, drywall with a denser core, known as *type X*, is used. Many different drywall and stud combinations may be fire rated. A common configuration for office construction uses one layer of 5/8" type X gypsum board on each side of a 2½" metal stud for a one-hour rating and two layers of 5/8" type X gypsum board for a two-hour rating. The full rated partition must run from floor to the underside of the floor above and any penetrations through the partition must be protected. Mechanical ductwork must have fire dampers and any doors must also be appropriately rated.

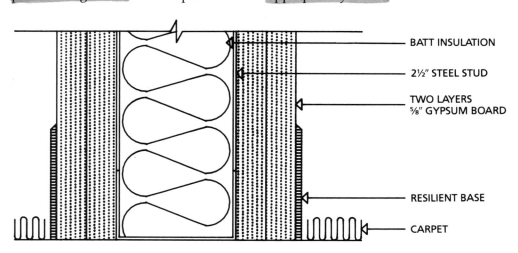

BATT INSULATION

2½" STEEL STUD

TWO LAYERS
⅝" GYPSUM BOARD

RESILIENT BASE

CARPET

ACOUSTICAL PARTITION DETAIL. The addition of batt insulation and extra layers of gypsum board will increase the STC rating.

Even though most interior office partitions do not require a fire rating, they usually must be noncombustible. Except as trim, wood may not be used unless it is fire treated.

Demountable Partitions

Demountable partitions are designed to be quickly and economically relocated with minimal waste or damage to surrounding construction. They may be constructed of gypsum drywall, metal panels, or other materials. Many furniture manufacturers provide demountable partitions as full-height versions of their open plan furniture system panels. Demountable partitions may qualify as movable furniture for tax and depreciation purposes. An accountant should be consulted if this is a consideration.

In drywall demountable partition systems, standard steel studs are replaced by steel or aluminum members shaped to anchor the drywall panels without the use of screws, tape, or spackle. Metal demountable partitions are made of prefabricated metal panels, generally with a honeycomb core for stiffness and sound control. Doors and frames are generally provided as integral parts of demountable partitions systems. Panels often come prefinished with a vinyl face, and integral glass panels are also available.

Demountable partitions are usually installed over carpet. When partitions are relocated, crushing of the carpet pile can be anticipated unless the carpet is extremely hard wearing. Carpet tiles are particularly appropriate for use in combination with demountable partitions. They are usually dense enough to resist showing wear when partitions are relocated—if not, they can be easily replaced.

Demountable partitions are anchored to ceiling construction and can damage ceiling tiles when relocated. This may be avoided by the use of special threaded ceiling tees designed to accept anchors from the demountable partition top track.

Demountable partitions work well in combination with raised access flooring. Demountable partitions encourage strictly modular space planning. This minimizes panels cut during the initial installation that cannot be reused and simplifies light fixture layout and ceiling and carpet repair.

Glass Partitions

Glass is a common partition material used to provide visual openness or to bring daylight into interior rooms. There are many ways to construct glass partitions. Frames may be constructed of steel, aluminum, or wood similar in detail to door frames. A frameless appearance may be achieved by setting the glass into recesses in the ceiling and adjoining partitions and by using shallow metal angles at the floor.

Glass partitions need not be full height. When used as a clerestory in a standard drywall partition, glass may allow natural light to penetrate into interior spaces while preserving privacy.

To avoid injury from glass shards, glass must usually be tempered or laminated. The use of untempered glass is usually restricted to very narrow openings. Glass may be clear or translucent in a variety of patterns and colors. Glass thicknesses range from 1/4" for small to average openings to 1/2" to 5/8" for large or unframed openings.

Another type of glass partition is made of glass block. Glass block is translucent, 4" to 8" thick, and installed like masonry with mortar joints.

Glass is generally not allowed in fire rated partitions or doors, except for wire glass or rated laminated glass in limited sizes.

DOORS, FRAMES, AND HARDWARE

Typical doors used in office construction are 1¾" thick by 3' 0" wide by full height; the top door frame being attached at the underside of the ceiling. Seven-foot-high doors are also common.

Traditionally, doors were made up of solid wood stiles and rails with small inset panels. While doors of this type are still available, the typical door for office construction today is a full flush panel with a flat seamless face of wood veneer or plastic laminate over a core made up of laminated solid wood blocks. Steel doors are also common and are usually full flush with a honeycomb core. When a fire rating is required a mineral core is used.

Unless made of stainless steel, steel doors are meant to be painted. Wood doors may have face veneers of birch or beech when the doors are intended to be painted or of oak, walnut, or other fine hardwood when a natural oil or transparent lacquer finish is desired. Plastic laminate is also used as a door-facing material.

Steel, aluminum, and wood are typical door frame materials. Steel frames, commonly called *hollow metal,* are made from flat sheets of steel, bent to shape. The bending causes corners to have a slight radius. Hollow metal frames may arrive on the job with the jambs and head welded into one piece or "knocked down" (KD) with jambs and head delivered as separate pieces. KD frames are less expensive and easier to handle but show a joint at the corners where the jambs meet the head, which may be aesthetically objectionable. Hollow metal door frames are usually painted.

Aluminum frames are extruded with square, sharp corners and anodized finishes in a natural silvery color or shades of gold, bronze, or black. Integrated aluminum door frames, window frames, and top and end caps are common components of demountable partition systems.

Wood frames are usually custom built in the field. Fire rated wood blocking is attached to the metal partition studs, the wood frame is attached to the blocking, and the joints between wood and drywall are covered with wood trim. Wood frames may have a painted or natural finish to match the door.

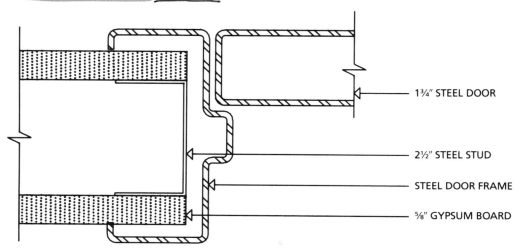

STEEL DOOR AND STEEL FRAME DETAIL. *A typical door jamb condition, used particularly when a fire rating is required.*

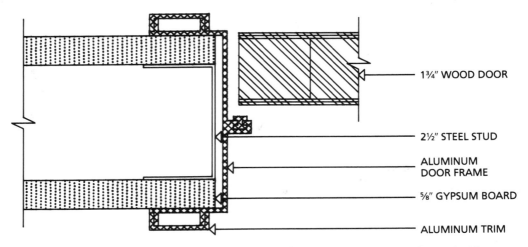

1¾″ WOOD DOOR

2½″ STEEL STUD

ALUMINUM DOOR FRAME

⅝″ GYPSUM BOARD

ALUMINUM TRIM

WOOD DOOR AND ALUMINUM FRAME DETAIL. Aluminum frames are also used with demountable partitions.

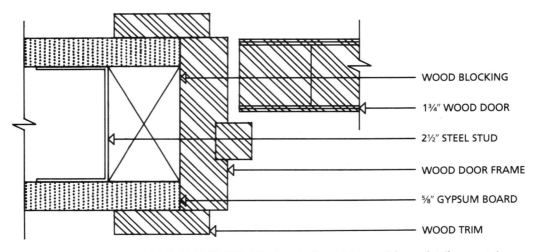

WOOD BLOCKING

1¾″ WOOD DOOR

2½″ STEEL STUD

WOOD DOOR FRAME

⅝″ GYPSUM BOARD

WOOD TRIM

WOOD DOOR AND WOOD FRAME DETAIL. A typical wood door and frame detail; many trim variations are possible.

Hollow metal frames are available with a fire rating. Wood and aluminum frames will not qualify for a fire rating unless used with a steel subframe.

Typical hardware for office doors consists of a latchset and strike plate, hinges, and a door stop. Levers are used instead of knobs to facilitate access for the disabled. Four mortised butt hinges, traditionally specified as *two pairs*, are generally required to support a full-height, solid-core door. For entry doors from public areas and for rooms with a security requirement, the latchset may be replaced by a lockset or a deadbolt may be used. Where doors require a fire rating, closers are required so that doors will come to rest in a closed position.

High-quality hardware is solid brass or stainless steel and available in a variety of finishes.

CEILINGS

In most office buildings ceilings are supported by a light metal grid suspended on wires from the floor structure above. Ceiling heights are generally 8' 6" to 9' 0" above the floor. The space between the ceiling and the floor above, usually a cavity about 2' 0" to 4' 0" deep in a modern high-rise office building, is filled with structural beams and joists, heating and air conditioning ductwork, housings for recessed lighting, sprinkler piping, electrical conduit and communications wiring. This crowded ceiling space also often acts as a plenum for air being recirculated back to the building air conditioning plant.

Smooth, monolithic ceilings are constructed of plaster on metal lath or drywall with a skim coat of plaster. Generally their use is limited to special areas, and they are particularly appropriate for soffits, vaulting, or other articulated ceilings. Since they lack the acoustical value of tile ceilings and are considerably more expensive, they are usually not used in general office areas. A major disadvantage is the difficulty of accessibility into the ceiling plenum, which is usually accomplished through the use of unattractive metal access panels built into the ceiling. To avoid cracking, expansion joints must be installed at approximately every thirty feet in each direction.

The most common ceiling material for commercial use is acoustical tile. Acoustical tiles may be made of a variety of materials including metal and glass fiber. Most tiles for office areas, however, are made of mineral fiber, 5/8" to 3/4" thick, available in a variety of surface patterns.

Acoustical tile systems may be either lay-in or concealed spline. Lay-in systems use an exposed, inverted T member of painted steel or aluminum within which an acoustical tile panel, typically 2' 0" by 4' 0" or 2' 0" by 2' 0", is placed. Such ceilings are easy to install and change and provide ready access to the ceiling plenum.

Acoustical tiles for concealed spline ceiling systems have kerfed edges into which the T support members are placed, thus hiding the grid from view. Tiles for concealed spline ceilings are generally 1' 0" by 1' 0" with square or beveled edges. Square edge tiles may give a smooth, seamless appearance initially, but, with time, slight irregularities that may be objectionable inevitably appear at the tile joints. Concealed spline ceilings are somewhat more expensive, more difficult to install, and plenum spaces are usually less accessible than with lay-in ceilings. However, they provide a clean, monolithic appearance.

As is obvious from its name, one function of an acoustical tile ceiling is to control sound. As the elements of the modern office interior evolved, acoustics played an important part. When acoustical tile ceilings replaced hard plaster, sound was absorbed rather than allowed to reflect back into the space.

Sound is measured in decibels (dB). Decibels are measured on a logarithmic scale. For example, 40 dB is twice as loud as 30 dB and 50 dB is twice as loud as 40 dB. Sound levels above 100 dB, such as that created by jet aircraft or rock music, may be physically painful and damaging to hearing. Absolute quiet is 0 dB and normal breathing is about 10 dB. Normal human speech at a normal conversational distance is in the range of 65 dB. The desirable background or ambient noise level in an open office area is in the 45 dB

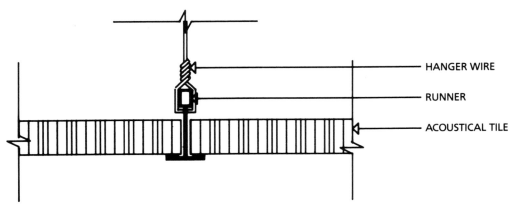

EXPOSED GRID CEILING DETAIL. An exposed grid may be used with 2' by 4' lay-in ceiling panels.

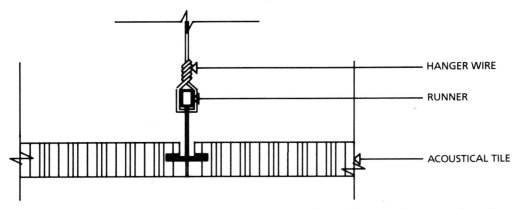

CONCEALED SPLINE CEILING DETAIL. Kerfed tiles (12" by 12") are used in a concealed spline ceiling system.

to 55 dB range. This sound is created by air conditioning fans, light fixture ballasts, office equipment, and people walking, talking, and shuffling papers, all moderated by the sound absorbing characteristics of acoustical tile, carpeting, and other materials. This background level means that normal conversations will usually not be overheard beyond ten to fifteen feet.

Acoustical tile ceilings help to maintain a desirable background noise level by absorbing sound. A measure of the ability of a material to absorb sound is known as its noise reduction coefficient (NRC). An NRC rating indicates the percentage of sound absorbed and is an average of the sound absorption coefficients of a material over the full range of frequencies. Hard surfaces, such as glass, plaster, and metal, reflect almost all sound and have NRC ratings close to 0. Mineral fiber acoustical tile will absorb about 75 percent of sound and thus has an NRC rating of 75. Low density glass fiber acoustical tile may have an NRC rating of 90.

Even with carpeting and acoustical tile, office spaces are often too noisy or too quiet and fine tuning is required. If the space is too noisy, solutions may involve adding sound absorbent material to the walls or hanging sound absorbent baffles from the ceiling. However, a more common problem in modern open office areas is too little background noise rather than too much. When the space is too quiet, privacy is lost. Common remedies are to add sound to the air conditioning system or to generate *white noise* through speakers placed above the ceiling.

Many acoustical problems can be solved empirically by architects or interior designers. When serious problems occur requiring accurate testing and complex solutions, the services of an acoustical consultant are recommended.

RAISED ACCESS FLOORING

With the advent of universal computerization, open plan workstations, and a desire for maximum flexibility in the office, a method was needed to distribute and reconfigure electrical and communication wiring quickly and economically. The solution was the raised access floor, which was initially developed for main frame computer rooms, but is increasingly being used in general office areas.

Raised access flooring consists of panels, usually two feet square, of steel, concrete, or a combination of the two. These are supported at their corners on posts that raise the panels from a few inches to up to two feet above the base building concrete slab. Electrical and communication wiring is run in the cavity thus formed. The panels are easily lifted to provide access. Holes are cut in the panels to allow wiring up to the workstation. Raised access flooring can be finished with resilient tile or carpet tiles.

Where raised access flooring meets the base building floor level, ramps must be provided. When it is determined before the building is constructed that raised access flooring will be needed, the base building floor slab can be depressed an appropriate amount to allow the raised access floor area to be level with the base building floor at elevator lobbies and toilet rooms.

WALL FINISHES

The most common wall finish for offices is paint. Synthetic latex paint is usually used on drywall. It applies easily, is cleaned up easily, and is relatively free of odor. Three coats of paint are usually specified, although dark colors may require an extra coat to cover properly.

Oil or alkyd based paint are commonly used for doors and architectural woodwork. They are more durable than latex paints but have an objectionable odor during application, and clean-up is more difficult. For an even tougher finish, enamels, epoxies, and lacquers may be used.

Paint can be applied in a variety of finishes from high gloss through semi-gloss to flat. High gloss and semi-gloss show surface irregularities but are easy to clean. Where high gloss paint is to be applied to drywall, a skim coat of plaster is sometimes used to level the surface. Flat paint hides surface blemishes but tends to show finger marks.

Paint is available in an infinite range of colors. Colors are significantly affected by the quality of light and final color selections should only be made under lighting identical to that which will be in the finished project. Paint samples for approval should be requested in the specifications and further inspections should be made of the actual application in the field.

Contractors should be asked to provide the client with several gallons of extra paint. This *attic stock* will be used for future touch-up work.

Wallcoverings include wallpaper, vinyl wallcoverings, and fabrics. They are applied to the wall surface with adhesive in vertical strips, usually 48" to 54" wide. They may also be *railroaded*, that is, applied horizontally. Wallcoverings should not terminate at outside corners where they can fray or peel back.

Vinyl wallcovering is available in a wide variety of finishes and weights from the thin, flat vinyl films used on the prefinished panels of demountable partition systems to heavy stipples and embossed patterns. While not very elegant, vinyl wallcovering provides a tough, easily cleaned wall surface. Although some vinyl wallcoverings are recoverable when pierced by pins or nails, when torn or cut the entire wall surface usually must be replaced.

Fabric wall coverings include linen, wool, silk, cotton, or other materials applied to a paper or vinyl backing to insure dimensional stability. They can be very expensive and are relatively fragile, but give a much softer and more luxurious feel than vinyl wallcoverings. Fabrics soil easily and should be given protection such as Scotchguard. Thin, delicate fabrics tend to show imperfections in the wall surface below.

A sophisticated application of wall fabric consists of fabric seamed into a large panel and stretched over a wood or metal frame applied to the wall surface. Batt insulation in the cavity absorbs sound. This installation conceals imperfections in the underlying wall surface and provides excellent acoustical properties.

Wallpaper is fragile and difficult to install. It is seldom used in commercial office interiors except in special, protected areas.

Most building codes require that wallcoverings be tested for flame spread, and most commercial wallcoverings carry labels listing their flame spread classification. Wallcoverings without a label should be avoided unless the client is willing to go through the time and expense of a test.

ARCHITECTURAL WOODWORK

If gypsum is the solid and dependable Beast of office construction, then wood is the Beauty. Common uses of wood in office projects in addition to softwood lumber for blocking and other construction include wood doors, wood flooring, furniture, and architectural woodwork such as paneling, trim, and built-in cabinets.

The characteristics of wood that should be considered by architects and interior designers in the selection of materials for architectural woodwork include species, figure and pattern, construction details, and finish.

Hardwood Species

The selection of a wood species for architectural woodwork depends primarily on the desired finished appearance and on cost and availability, which can vary widely from species to species and year to year. Oak, walnut, cherry, maple, and ash are domestic hardwoods suitable for natural finishing. Redwood is a softwood occasionally found in interiors. Birch and beech are hardwoods that may have a natural finish but are more commonly painted.

Teak, mahogany, and rosewood are tropical hardwoods. While many tropical hardwoods come from sustained-yield forests, there is concern over the ecological effects of the destruction of tropical rain forests that affects the supply and acceptability of some of these woods.

Obviously not a hardwood but used in similar ways, plastic laminate is made of layers of kraft paper laminated with resins under high heat and pressure to a decorative colored or patterned face sheet. High pressure plastic laminate is a very hard material suitable for counter-tops, doors, and other areas subject to abuse. Medium pressure laminate is suitable for vertical paneling applications.

Figure and Pattern

Solid wood is used for trim, but paneling and the tops and faces of cabinets are usually constructed of veneers laminated to plywood or particle board cores. Veneers are generally 1/28" to 1/42" thick. The grain figure in the veneer is largely a matter of how the veneer is cut from the log. Common cuts are rotary cut, plain sliced, quarter sliced, and rift cut. Another cut is composite veneer, often used for open plan furniture systems.

❏ Rotary peeling is the most common and economical of veneer cuts, although the grain is inconsistent and difficult to match. In rotary peeling the log is rotated against the veneer knife, creating a continuous veneer sheet as the knife spirals its way into the center of the log. Rotary peeling is used with softwood to make the plies for plywood. When used for hardwood veneers, it is best suited for paint grade finishes.

❏ In plain slicing or flat cutting, the knife cuts straight through the log from top to bottom, creating a series of easily matched veneer leaves with a cathedral-like grain pattern.

❏ In quarter slicing the log is first cut into quarters. The knife then cuts veneer leaves parallel to a radius cut through the center of the quarter-log. Quarter slicing produces a straight grained figure but is more expensive than plain slicing.

❏ Quarter slicing of oak may result in the appearance of *flake*, considered a blemish, caused by the radial medullary rays of the wood. This may be avoided by rift cutting. In rift cutting, a quartered log is rotated against the veneer knife, slicing across the medullary rays.

❏ Composite veneer is made from veneers that have been rotary sliced, then stacked and glued together into a block. These blocks are sliced at an angle to make sheets of veneer. Veneers made in this way have the controlled, consistent grain pattern required for open plan furniture systems where furniture panels must be installed and subsequently reconfigured without regard to grain matching.

Except for rotary cutting, natural veneer leaves range from 5" to 10" in width. Once cut from the log, they are laid side by side to create the finished panel. For veneers to be painted or veneers with very straight grain, such as rift cut oak, the order of laying up the veneers makes little difference. For veneers with a bold figure, the final appearance will vary greatly depending on the pattern selected for assembling the flitches. Methods of matching between adjacent veneer leaves include book matching, slip matching, random matching, and end matching.

❏ Book matching has every other veneer leaf turned over to match as in the pages of a book. The pattern results in a distinctive "butterfly" effect.

❏ Slip matching has veneer leaves arranged in sequence with all exposing the same side.

❏ Random matching varies the veneer leaves, randomly resulting in a casual, board-like appearance.

❏ End matching is book matching veneer leaves end-to-end as well as side-to-side.

Veneers may be laminated to plywood or particle board. Plywood is made of thin layers of wood with alternate layers arranged with the grain at right angles to provide strength and dimensional stability. Particle board is made from sawdust or wood chips bound together with resins. It is more dimensionally stable than plywood but is usually heavier and does not hold nails and screws as well.

Where the edges of a sheet of veneered plywood will be exposed, edge banding must be applied. The least-expensive process, but most easily damaged, is to veneer the plywood edges. Better results are obtained when a piece of hardwood of the same species as the face veneer is applied to the edge.

Construction

To insure that the desired design effect is achieved, architects and interior designers should provide elevations and complete details of all important joinery conditions of architectural woodwork on the construction documents. The architectural woodworking contractor will take field dimensions and prepare shop drawings, usually full-size, showing every detail condition. These drawings are then checked by both the general contractor and architect or interior designer against the construction drawings. The architectural woodworking contractor is responsible for scribing, shimming, and otherwise conforming to field conditions.

Wood paneling may be constructed and applied in a variety of ways. The simplest, least expensive, but least satisfactory aesthetically is to laminate wood veneer to a flexible fabric backing and apply it to the wall surface like wallpaper. A second method is to laminate veneer to 1/4" plywood that is glued to the wall surface in panels. Edges may be covered with trim or left exposed with narrow painted *reveals* between adjacent panels. The most expensive but highest-quality wood paneling is produced with veneer on thick plywood panels, precisely located and suspended from the wall surface on metal clips.

Wood Finishes

Typical wood finishes are paint, natural oil, or lacquer. Paint may be enamel with an oil base or latex with flat, semi-gloss, or gloss finish. For a natural finish, the color may be varied with stains that lighten, darken, even out, or tint the natural wood color. Aniline dyes provide a colored surface similar to paint while allowing the grain to remain visible.

A finish coat of oil, lacquer, or polyurethane may be applied over the stained or dyed wood. Natural oil is a fairly fragile finish and must be reapplied periodically. Synthetic or natural lacquer, either flat, semi-gloss, or high gloss, provides a clear, thin, durable finish. For a distinctive thick, glass-like finish for countertops or other wearing surfaces, a thick coat of clear polyurethane may be used.

WOOD FLOORING

Wood flooring is made of hardwood such as oak, walnut, or maple. Strip and plank flooring is made of random length, tongue and grooved strips 2¼" wide or planks 3" to 5" wide by 3/4" thick. Parquet flooring is wood laid in geometric patterns, often with a mixture of wood species to give color variation.

Wood flooring may be used by itself or in combination with area rugs or other materials. Wood flooring may be used as a border around a room with carpeting inset in the center, or the process may be reversed, with areas of wood flooring set into a field of carpet to provide a hard wearing surface at a desk for chair casters.

Wood flooring may be applied directly to the concrete floor with mastic or may be applied over a plywood underlayment. Flooring over underlayment gives a more level, higher-quality, and more expensive installation. Total floor thickness, however, may be as much as 1½", so special care must be taken at elevator door thresholds and transitions to other flooring materials.

Wood flooring expands and contracts depending on humidity conditions, and expansion gaps should be allowed at the perimeter.

Wood flooring may be stained to change color or even out the color. The final finish is usually a hard polyurethane. Wood flooring requires frequent care to maintain its appearance.

CERAMIC TILE

Ceramic tile is made from clay that has been fired at a high temperature to create a hard, impervious material. It is used on floors and walls, commonly in such wet areas as kitchens and bathrooms. Three types of ceramic tile are glazed ceramic tile, vitreous tile, and quarry tile.

❏ Glazed ceramic tile is fired twice, first the tile body alone then the tile with an applied glaze. It generally has a smooth, high-gloss finish and is available in almost any color and many patterns. It is slippery when wet and not resistant to abrasion. It comes in many sizes with 4¼" square being the most common. Thickness is typically 5/16" to 3/8".

❏ Vitreous or mosaic tile is fired once, resulting in integral color and a matte finish. Common sizes are 1/4" thick by 1" or 2" square.

❏ Quarry tile is a rugged tile suitable for hard use such as commercial kitchens. It is unglazed with integral color, generally in gray and brown earth tones. Standard quarry tile is 6" square by 1/2" thick. Abrasive grit may be embedded in the surface to increase slip resistance.

The traditional method of installing ceramic tile is in a cement mortar bed, 3/4" to 1" thick. When installed on the wall, the mortar is applied to wire or expanded metal lath and the joints are grouted with a cement-lime mixture. This installation method gives the highest-quality result.

Today, however, most ceramic tile is installed by the thin-set method. The tile is set into a thin adhesive that is applied over a water-resistant base material. A cement-lime grout is used to fill the joints.

Mortar-set tile is more expensive than thin-set tile. It is also much thicker. When used adjacent to other materials such as carpet, either the carpet must be raised up on a plywood or other base, a reducing threshold must be used, or the bordering tiles must slope down to meet the carpet.

STONE

Stone is one of the oldest and most durable construction materials. While basically structural, its use today is primarily as a surfacing material for buildings, both exterior and interior. In office interiors stone is used for decorative flooring and, less frequently, as a wall surface material. Stone reflects sound and is hard underfoot, which makes it impractical for most working areas. Its attractive characteristics of color and grain, however, make it appropriate for such special, ceremonial areas as lobbies or galleries. Stone is among the most expensive interior finish materials. Stone most frequently used for flooring includes granite, travertine, marble, and slate.

❏ Granite is an igneous stone created by the cooling of molten rock into a crystalline structure of great strength and hardness. Granite usually has a fine, speckled appearance and comes in many colors from black through red, green, and gray to white.

❏ Sedimentary rock is formed of deposits of silt, sand, or tiny calcium bearing sea organisms acted on by heat, pressure, and chemical action. Over time, the result is limestone or sandstone, common as exterior building materials, but usually too soft for flooring. One form of limestone used in interiors is travertine, which is created by the evaporation of water from hot springs. It exhibits characteristic small open pores and a creamy yellow to white color. To resist soiling, the pores may be filled with Portland cement or epoxy.

❏ Marble is a metamorphic rock, a sedimentary rock further acted on by heat and pressure until a hard, crystalline structure is formed. Marble is softer and more porous than granite and exhibits an irregular grain pattern. Marble comes in pure white and a wide variety of other colors.

❏ Slate is a hard, fine-grained, stratified metamorphic stone, typically black in color.

Stone is selected by color and pattern from samples of the exact material proposed for the project. As a natural material, a range of variation from the selected color and pattern is to be expected, and samples submitted by contractors for approval should reflect the extremes of this range. The architect or interior designer may also want to visit the quarry to select the actual stone to be used on the project.

Stone for flooring is cut to size and installed according to the pattern specified by the architect or interior designer. The larger the size of each stone, the thicker it must be to avoid cracking under impact. Maximum sizes usually do not exceed two feet square with a thickness of 3/4" to 1".

Stone flooring is usually set in a bed of mortar resulting in a total thickness of approximately 1½". Care must be taken that there are no voids in the setting bed that may allow cracking of the stone. Unless the floor has been specifically recessed to accept the stone flooring during the construction of the building, sloped edge details will be required where the stone meets elevator door thresholds and other flooring materials.

Stone may be polished to a high gloss or honed to a matte finish. A high gloss finish may be too slippery for safety. Granite is also available in a flamed finish where the surface is spalled off by an acetylene torch leaving an even, pebbly surface.

LIGHTING

A common light fixture provided by landlords for standard tenant construction is a three or four tube, 2' 0" by 4' 0" recessed fluorescent fixture with an acrylic lens, furnished in quantities of one fixture per 75 to 90 square feet of floor area. This will provide light at a desktop in the range of 70 to 100 footcandles, sufficient for most office tasks. These fixtures are often air-handling, that is, they are provided with slots around their perimeter that can be connected to HVAC ductwork for air supply or left open to allow return air into the ceiling plenum.

Recessed fluorescent fixtures are supported on the same grid that supports the acoustical tile ceiling. In a 2' 0" by 4' 0" lay-in ceiling, fixtures should follow the grid pattern. In a 12" by 12" concealed spline ceiling, fluorescent fixtures should follow the layout of the main runner channels supporting the ceiling.

Fluorescent fixtures are available with many variations. Other common fixture sizes are 2' 0" by 2' 0" and 1' 0" by 4' 0". Parabolic louvers are often used instead of acrylic lenses. These are plastic or metal grids that can range in size from 3/4" square to 12" square with a parabolic profile that directs light down to the worksurface more efficiently than an acrylic lens. They are usually finished in a polished chrome or gold color. These create what is known as *low brightness* fixtures because they appear dark on the ceiling plane.

Landlords often specify the type of lamp to be used in fluorescent fixtures to insure that the building has a uniform appearance from the exterior and to simplify the stocking of replacement lamps. Fluorescent lamps come in a wide variety of colors, such as cool white and warm white. The lamp color significantly affects the appearance of the colors of furniture and other materials, and these finishes should be selected using the lamps that will be in the project.

Fluorescent lighting is powered by electrical wiring in circuits of approximately ten fixtures each from an electrical panel located in the electrical closet in the building core. Light switching for each circuit is usually done by room or by zone for large open work areas and corridors. Automatic switching is an option. Automatic switching may be by time clock, by photocells that turn the lights on when outside light becomes too dim, or by occupancy sensors that detect movement and turn the fixtures off when a room is unoccupied. Dimmers are available for fluorescent fixtures.

Computers provide a challenge in lighting design. Since computer screens are self-lighted, no external light is required to see the screen. Normal office lighting can cause glare on computer screens, so a low level of overall light is preferred. For working with printed reference material, however, a relatively high level of light is needed. The problem is that computer operators often simultaneously work with both. A solution is the *task light*. This is nothing more than an old-fashioned table lamp, either incandescent or fluorescent, often mounted on the underside of overhead storage units or at the end of a flexible arm.

Ambient lighting, one solution to the problem of glare, is basically a light fixture turned upside down and installed on the top of an open plan workstation or a free-standing pedestal at a height of approximately six feet. The light shines up to the white acoustical tile ceiling where it is evenly diffused.

Incandescent lighting in office space is usually reserved for accent lighting for special areas. While the light quality is high, incandescent fixtures are more costly, use significantly more electricity, and generate more heat than fluorescent fixtures. Common fixtures are recessed downlights or wall washers with parabolic reflectors. Fixture spacing depends on the amount of light required and the wattage of the bulb used. Recessed fixtures may extend 12" into the ceiling cavity and should be checked against the location of structure and ductwork to avoid interference.

Perhaps no technical aspect of office design is currently undergoing as much change as lighting. Driven by the need for energy conservation, a myriad of new fixtures and techniques are being developed. Among these are compact fluorescents, low voltage lamps, miniature reflector (MR) incandescents, tungsten halogen lamps, and high intensity discharge (HID) lamps. Great improvements have also been made in the energy-saving and color-rendering characteristics of fluorescent lamps.

POWER AND
COMMUNICATIONS WIRING

Electrical power is distributed to each workplace from a panel located in an electrical closet at the building core. This power is divided into a number of circuits, originating at a circuit breaker in the panel and providing 110 volt power to between ten to thirty outlets. Separate circuits are used where 220 volt power is needed or where equipment requires "clean" power. Communication wiring may be similarly distributed from dedicated core spaces.

One method of distribution is through the use of raised access flooring. Other methods include poke-through, underfloor ducts, wall outlets, and flat tape.

❑ In the <u>poke-through method</u>, power and communication wiring is distributed through the ceiling of the space below. The floor slab is cored and wires run to outlets in monuments anchored to the floor. Electrical wiring must be run in conduit for fire protection. Conduit may not be needed for communications wiring, however, if it is coated with a tough, fireproofing material such as Teflon. Since this method requires access to the ceiling of the floor below, installation may be difficult if a tenant occupies that space.

INCONVINENCE TO PEOPLE BELOW

❑ Some high-rise office buildings are designed to distribute power and communication wiring to tenants through underfloor ducts. These are corrugations in the steel formwork used to create the concrete floor slab that have been en-

UNDER FLOOR DUCTS

"DUCT"

closed by a flat steel plate. The floor is cored into these underfloor ducts and wiring run to outlets in floor monuments. Since the underfloor ducts are enclosed, conduit is not required and there is no disturbance to the tenants on the floor below. For buildings so designed, this is the least expensive and most efficient way to provide power to tenants and will be the method favored in the lease workletter.

❑ Electrical and communication wiring may be distributed above the ceiling and through conduit inside office partitions to wall outlets. As with the poke-through method, conduit is required above the ceiling for electrical wiring but may be omitted for communications wiring if a Teflon coating is used. This method works well for private offices but not for open plan workstations.

✓ CARPET TILES

❑ Flat tape may be used to provide power and communication wiring to open plan workstations. Special junction boxes are installed at a partition and a flat tape of sandwich construction containing the wiring is run under the carpeting to floor monuments. This method may only be used with carpet tiles. It is very flexible but relatively expensive.

HEATING, VENTILATING,
AND AIR CONDITIONING

Office space is maintained at its desired temperature through the movement of heated or cooled air. Two common methods for delivering this air are diffusion at the ceiling or by the use of convectors or fan coil units at the perimeter.

For diffusion at the ceiling, air that has been heated or cooled in a central plant either on the floor or elsewhere in the building is routed through galvanized steel ductwork to ceiling diffusers or to perimeter slots in air-handling light fixtures. After circulating in the space, the air is returned to the ceiling cavity or plenum through grilles in the ceiling or through open slots in the light fixtures, there to find its way back to the central plant where the process starts all over again. At the central plant the air is also humidified, filtered, and mixed with a proportion of outside air.

Office building floors are typically divided into zones for heating, ventilating, and air conditioning (HVAC); each zone is controlled by a thermostat. Each thermostat regulates the amount and/or temperature of the air delivered to one or more diffuser locations by adjusting the output of mixing boxes located within the ceiling cavity. At the perimeter of the floor each zone may cover 150 to 400 square feet and include 10' to 20' of window. Interior zones may be much larger.

Heating and cooling of perimeter zones may also be accomplished by convectors or fan coil units located at the windows. Hot or cold water is delivered to these units through finned pipes. Air passing over the fins is, respectively, heated or cooled and then circulated through the room by fans in fan coil units or by natural convection currents. Units are usually located directly under windows to partly counter the effects of outside temperature on the glass.

Energy conservation policies adopted in the 1970s as a result of the oil crisis required that thermostats be raised in the summer and lowered in the winter. These policies also produced buildings that were more tightly sealed against outside air. One of the results has been a lack of ventilation leading to a deterioration of indoor air quality, or the *sick building syndrome*, which can cause illness among office workers. The introduction of a much greater volume of fresh, outside air is one part of the solution.

Computers have a particular sensitivity to air temperature, which the base building HVAC system may not be able to satisfy. Large computer systems may require twenty-four-hour cooling from separate stand-alone systems.

CHAPTER TEN

FURNISHINGS

The determination of requirements, and the selection, specification, and procurement of new furnishings is a part of most office projects. The architect or interior designer is usually responsible for most of this process.

The distinction between furniture and construction is often arbitrary. One difference might be defined by portability. Furniture is personal property, not attached to the premises, and may be removed by the tenant at the expiration of the lease. Construction is a capital improvement, attached to the premises, and is ultimately the property of the landlord. This may have tax as well as lease and ownership implications. A credenza, for example, may be considered furniture if free standing; if attached to a partition it becomes construction. Electrified furniture panels in open plan workstations may be considered as permanently attached when hardwired to the building's electrical distribution system.

Another distinction between construction and furnishings might depend on who performs the work. This distinction may determine where various items are shown on drawings and how they are specified and organized into bid packages. General contractors provide construction, while carpet and furniture are typically purchased from their respective dealers. A custom-designed credenza,

if built by a manufacturer and installed by a dealer, is furniture; if constructed and installed by a millwork shop working for the general contractor, it is construction.

During the programming phase it is convenient to think of a project as a collection of planning units, each planning unit being a logical grouping of related job functions often corresponding to a department, division, or section in the client's organization chart. Each planning unit requires a defined amount of floor space and is located in the project in the space plan.

In the programming phase, preliminary workplace standards are used. While these are intended to be accurate enough to develop planning unit requirements, they are not the result of in-depth analysis and usually must be further modified to meet actual, specific needs. Typically it is during the schematic design or design development phase that detailed workplace requirements are determined and furniture selected.

Just as the project is made up of a number of planning units, each planning unit may be thought of as being a collection of workplaces. A workplace may be defined as any logical, small grouping of furnishings and equipment that fulfills a specific job function and is generally, although not necessarily, occupied by one person. Whether for the selection and specification of new furnishings or for the relocation of existing furnishings, the workplace grouping is a useful organizing and tracking device.

A workplace may take many forms. It may be a private office, open plan workstation, or open desk arrangement for an individual office worker. It may be a reception room, conference room, or other departmental or planning unit support area. It may be a bank of files, coffee station, or even a grouping of planters that acts as a space divider.

The determination of workplace requirements may be accomplished through replication of existing workplaces, an analysis of job function, a survey of employee needs, or a combination of all three.

The simplest method for determining workplace requirements is to replicate existing conditions. This method is appropriate when existing furnishings and equipment are to be reused or when existing configurations are to be duplicated with new furnishings.

At the other extreme, workplace requirements may begin with an analysis of the job function itself rather than its furnishings and equipment, that is, by finding out what workers do, rather than what they want. Some architects and interior designers believe this approach yields more objective information. Others feel this method is too complex and time consuming and that the results seldom justify the extra effort.

This approach may be appropriate, however, if the job function is a new one

in the company or if it is undergoing major change, such as computerization. Detailed job function analysis may be beyond the scope of design firm expertise and require the involvement of management consultants or computer specialists. Job function analysis is also used by furniture designers in researching new workstation designs.

Job function analysis may involve observation of employees at work, surveys, and interviews. One device is the diary where, for a period of a week or two, each employee is asked to record exactly what he or she is doing minute by minute. A computer analysis can then provide an accurate profile of worker activities that may then be translated by the architect or interior designer into furnishings selections.

A method midway between replication of existing conditions and analysis of job function is to survey employee requirements by simply asking people what they need. Initially a written survey may be used to discover basic information. However, to develop a feel for the requirements, a face-to-face interview is usually also desirable. Each employee may be asked for a description of the furnishings and equipment necessary or desirable for his or her job function. These requirements are then reviewed and confirmed by the planning unit heads. For large projects, a separate meeting with every person is usually impractical and representative employees of each job function are selected for interviews.

The survey or interview begins with an identification of the job title and a description of the job function. Specific elements of the workplace to be determined include worksurface, storage, seating, equipment, accessories, display, privacy, and security:

Worksurface: How much worksurface area is required for reading, writing, drawing, drafting, sorting, or filing? How much is required for conferencing? How much is required for a telephone, personal computer, and other equipment? How much is required for active storage and reference material? How much is required for such personal artifacts as a spouse's picture or vase of flowers? Is any worksurface, such as a conference area, shared between workplaces?

Storage: How much storage is required for files? What size are the files? How much shelving is required for books and binders? How much cabinet or drawer storage is required for supplies and miscellaneous material? Is a specialized stationery drawer or pencil drawer required? Are fire-resistant files or cabinets required? Is a coat closet required? Is any storage shared between workplaces?

Seating: What type and how much seating is required for the workplace occupant? How much guest seating is required? How much informal or lounge seating is required.

Equipment: What type of computer equipment is required? Where should it be located? Is a printer required at the workplace? What type of communicating equipment is used, such as telephone, speaker telephone, or facsimile device? What other equipment, such as a typewriter or audio-visual equipment, is located at the workplace? Is equipment shared between workplaces?

Accessories: What type of accessories, such as a deskpad, letter tray, pencil cup, pen set, wastebasket, memo pad, calendar, index file, or ashtray, are required?

Display: Are tackboards, chalkboards, markerboards, flip charts, or projection screens required? What provision for artwork or personal artifacts is needed?

Privacy: What degree of visual privacy is required? What degree of acoustical privacy is required? Must the workplace be visible to maintain supervisory control?

Security: Which, if any, drawers and file cabinets require locks? Does the workplace itself require a locked door?

With suitable modifications, these questions are applicable for conference rooms, workrooms, storage areas, libraries, and other workplaces on the project. As with all interviews, the information gathered should be dated, identified as to author and interviewee, sent to the interviewee for confirmation, and reviewed and approved by client management.

Once gathered, the information must be analyzed. From a great many titles and job functions certain patterns and similarities will emerge. In most client organizations employee workplaces can be grouped into fewer than ten generic types, even including those with highly specialized requirements. Most conference, work, and storage rooms can be similarly standardized.

Each generic workplace can be identified by a distinctive code, such as A, B, C, and defined by an assigned square footage and list of furnishings and equipment. Slight variations in requirements can be designated by subnumbers, such as D1, D2, D3. This subnumbering will also accommodate variations owing to planning and design.

FURNITURE SELECTION

Once requirements are established, furniture may be selected to meet that criteria.

WORKPLACE REQUIREMENTS SURVEY

Project:	Tyrell Corporation/Operations Center
Workplace:	Accounting Supervisor
Code:	D1
Area:	100 square feet
Worksurface:	Standard surface for reading, writing, etc., and conferencing for 3 people Standard surface for reference material, etc. Surface for personal computer
Storage:	4 legal file drawers 6' of book shelving for 8½" × 11" binders 1 box drawer 1 pencil drawer
Seating:	Desk chair 2 guest chairs
Equipment:	Telephone FAX Personal computer
Display:	None
Privacy:	Moderate acoustical privacy Moderate visual privacy
Security:	Files must be locked
Accessories:	Double letter tray Wastebasket
Other:	
By:	J. S. Sebastian
Date:	11/5/—
Approved:	Eldon Tyrell
Date:	11/21/—

WORKPLACE REQUIREMENTS SURVEY. This survey may be distributed to users for completion or filled out by the architect or interior designer during user interviews.

There are several sources for furniture. On almost every project some will be existing—used furniture to be moved from its present location into the new offices. Some furnishings will be new, selected specifically for the project. Finally, furnishings might be specified from an inventory or list of existing corporate standards.

From the thousands of products available in the marketplace, only a few will be appropriate for any given project. Criteria should be established against which each piece of furniture can be evaluated. Some of these criteria include:

Design: Is the furniture consistent with the design concept? Are desired colors and finishes available?

Quality: Is the furniture well constructed? Will it be reliable over the long term? What maintenance is required?

Budget: Will the cost of the furniture meet the budget? Will future orders of the same furniture or components be reasonably priced?

Function: Does the furniture meet the functional criteria established for each workplace type? What options and variations are available?

Availability: Can the furniture be provided on time? Can future orders of the same furniture or components be provided in a reasonable time?

Safety: Does the furniture meet appropriate codes and standards for flammability, stability, and other safety criteria?

Manufacturer dependability: Will the manufacturer produce the furniture as promised? Is the manufacturer financial-

ly stable? Will additional furniture or components of the same design be available in the future?

Vendor dependability: Will the vendor perform as promised? Is the vendor financially stable? What are the vendor's management capabilities? How good are the vendor's installation crews? Will the vendor promptly correct errors and damage? What are the vendor's warehousing capabilities?

For open plan workstation systems, additional criteria are needed:

Flexibility: Can the workstation be easily reconfigured? Are a wide variety of components available?

Wire management: How is electrical and communications wiring managed within the system? How compatible is it with building wiring distribution? How does the system accommodate task or ambient lighting?

The search for appropriate furniture usually begins with catalogs and price lists. Product and finishes libraries for interior planning and design work are far more extensive than for building core and shell design. Experienced architects and interior designers can usually quickly identify most of the products appropriate for a given project. Without experience, searching through the mass of information available can be an arduous process. Trade magazines, visits to showrooms and presentations by manufacturers' representatives are necessary to keep informed of what's available. To see the widest variety of products, visits to major market locations, such as Chicago, New York, or Los Angeles, may be helpful.

Usually the first pass at furniture selection can reduce the thousands of products available to less than a dozen of each type. At this point examination of actual samples may be desirable. Since furniture is a manufactured product, the actual items are almost always available for examination, although colors and finishes may vary.

Manufactured furniture is frequently not available in the desired finish from the manufacturers standard line. This may require the use of what is known as customer's own material (COM). This is typical for items using fabric or leather, such as seating or panels for open plan workstation systems. This adds a level of complication to the furniture acquisition process. It also will complicate future orders of the same furniture or components. The fabric must be ordered from a separate vendor and approved by the seating or workstation manufacturer for suitability for the end product. Fire ratings must be checked. Once ordered, samples must be approved and the goods shipped to the seating or workstation manufacture for final inclusion in the product. There are many things that can go wrong and the process must be carefully coordinated. While this coordination is the responsibility of the furniture contractor, the architect or interior designer inevitably becomes deeply involved.

Open Plan Systems Furniture

The work of George Nelson in the 1940s and 1950s with component furniture and storage walls, the invention by Robert Probst in the 1960s of the Herman Miller Action Office furniture system, and the development of Series 9000 by Steelcase in the 1970s, introduced a new concept in office furniture, a system of components that would provide open area privacy, utilize vertical space, and be easily recon-

figured to meet the changing needs of the user. Systems furniture accomplishes many things. Panels of various heights can support worksurfaces and storage units, as well as provide privacy. Electrical and communication wiring can be integrated within panels. Systems furniture is flexible and can be easily moved or rearranged. It can be personalized with a wide selection of options to suit a variety of functional needs.

There are hundreds of furniture systems available in the marketplace. They differ in appearance, materials, quality, price, availability, and variety and type of components. From a space planning standpoint, however, the most critical variation is in dimension. Systems work on different dimensional modules and a layout based on one system will generally have to be revised if another system is chosen. Clearances and passageway widths may change and different quantities of workstations may be accommodated in the same overall space simply because of minor dimensional variations between products.

Because of these planning implications, a workstation system is often selected during the design phases of a project, far in advance of the normal purchasing process. Bids may be solicited on a unit price basis based on preliminary workstation configurations and estimated quantities. A letter of intent may be written for the selected system, and purchase agreements only executed when final configurations and quantities are determined. This process has the added advantage of being able to utilize the technical capabilities of the system's manufacturer in the design and preparation of documents.

For large projects, mock-ups of open plan workstations in some or all required configurations may be installed in the client's existing premises. This allows clients to visualize and test the workstation under actual operating conditions. Such mock-ups are expensive and manufacturers may expect to be compensated, particularly if custom items are required. They also take time. If a mock-up will be needed, manufacturers need adequate time to prepare, sometimes several months.

Filing

In "office of the future" theories of the 1970s and 1980s, the computer was supposed to result in the paperless office. Instead, paper has proliferated. People feel comfortable working with paper, and it is unlikely that it will disappear in the near future.

Paper may be categorized by accessibility. The most accessible are the personal papers and files in the individual workplace. Next are the files located within each planning unit and used by its personnel. Third are general files located in designated separate areas or file rooms. Finally there are dead files that may be located off-premises. It is important that these categories be clearly distinguished during programming and workplace requirements surveys.

Paper may also be categorized by type and size. The most common form of paper storage is the letter-size or legal-size file. Paper may also be stored in binders of various sorts. The computer has spawned computer printouts, often much larger than legal paper, drawings of various sizes may need to be stored, and, in addition to paper, there may be requirements for disk and tape storage for the computer. Each type of paper or other medium requires specialized storage furniture. For flexibility, it is advisable to standardize the type and size of this furniture as much as possible.

The most common storage furniture is the file cabinet. Vertical file cabinets are accessed at their short dimension and lateral files are accessed at their long dimension. Standard file drawers are approximately 12" high. A two-drawer file cabinet is approximately desk height and a three-drawer cabinet is stand-up work counter height. The top surface of a four-drawer file cabinet is inconvenient for work and the more efficient five-drawer cabinet is usually preferable. Five drawers is the usual maximum for convenient access and storage. Above that height, cabinets are usually in the form of overfile storage units. For ease of access, the upper drawers of a lateral file cabinet usually have flipper doors and roll-out shelves.

Cabinets for letter files are approximately 15" wide and those for legal files approximately 18" wide. Since they can accommodate both letter and legal files, legal-size file cabinets are more flexible.
If security is required, locks may be specified. File cabinets that are resistant to fire are available. They are usually somewhat larger than nonrated cabinets owing to the thickness of the fireproofing material in the walls. The interior arrangement of file cabinets also need to be specified as to compressors, hanging file frames, or other options.

Loaded five-drawer file cabinets with overfile storage, particularly when banked together, may approach the maximum allowable structural floor loading and should be checked by a structural engineer.

Banks of file cabinets are often installed in specially constructed niches. Since dimensions vary slightly by manufacturer and model, the exact file cabinet needs to be determined before the niche is dimensioned. Extra clearance should be allowed in the width, depth, and height of the niche as a margin of safety. If desired, the space between the file cabinets and the niche walls and ceiling may be filled with a shim strip or covered by trim.

Seating

The primary criteria for the selection of seating is the way it supports the human body. The design and manufacture of seating to meet these requirements is based upon principles of human factors or *ergonomics*, the study of the interaction between people and their environment. Ergonomically designed furnishings, particularly seating, are intended to provide comfort, promote health, and prevent injury.

Chair seatpans and backs should be adjustable and shaped and cushioned to properly support the back, arms, buttocks, and legs. They should not cause pressure that can restrict blood circulation or pinch nerves. Seat depth should not be so deep as to cause pressure behind the knee. Chairs should tilt, swivel, and move easily on casters to allow the body to change position frequently. Seat height should be adjustable. Adjustment should be easy to accomplish by the worker. The base, typically five-star, should prevent the chair from being easily overturned. Optional enhancements may include armrest adjustment and linked adjustment of seatpan, back, and armrests.

More than any other category of furniture, seating, particularly desk chairs, should never be purchased without first being tried out by the users. If samples cannot be brought to the design firm or tenant's existing offices, showroom visits should be arranged. People in the office sit in their chairs from four to eight hours a day. They must kept safe, healthy, and comfortable.

FURNITURE AND EQUIPMENT INVENTORIES

When existing furnishings and equipment are to be reused, a formal inventory is usually needed. This is the responsibility of the client and many companies maintain current inventories as part of asset management programs. If such documentation does not exist, an inventory may be performed by the client, by the design team as an additional service, or by a furniture dealer or other consultant.

The physical inventory begins with a walk-through of the existing offices. A floor plan of the existing office space is useful for note taking and reference. If one does not exist, it may be advantageous to sketch one.

A catalog page may be created for each unique item. This may contain a code and identifying name, a Polaroid photograph, the manufacturer and model number, the size, weight, material, color, and finish and comments concerning condition. A summary sheet may also be prepared that shows the quantity of each cataloged item and the present location of each piece. A sticker showing the identifying code is often placed in an inconspicuous, but standardized, location on each item. Many companies use a computerized bar coding system for this purpose. This may be integrated into the design firm's CADD data base.

Specialized inventories may be desirable. An inventory of filing, for example, may be more than a count of filing cabinets. It may be useful to know the quantity of files of each type, usually measured in terms of *filing inches*. Similar studies may be done for paper and supplies, library books, and periodicals. An office move is a good time for a dead filing, file reduction, or purge campaign or for a reevaluation of supply backlog.

Furnishings to be reused may need

EQUIPMENT INVENTORY

Project:	Tyrell Corporation/Operations Center
Item:	HAL/Laser Printer Model LPS8
Dimensions:	19″ wide × 17″ deep × 12″ high Desktop
Clearances:	8″ left side 6″ right side 6″ rear 12″ front
Weight:	44 #
Operation:	Continuous forms and single sheets feed from top rear
Communication:	Data cable length, 25′ (Allowable maximum cable length, 2000′)
Mechanical:	Maximum heat dissipation, 690 BTU/hr
Electrical:	Operating AC power, 220 volt amps Start-up AC power, 780 volt amps Nominal AC Supply voltage, 115/220 VAC, separate circuit, 50/60 hz Power cable length, 10′ NEMA power receptacle, 5-151G
Plumbing:	None
Vendor:	Nitro-Chemical Corporation Los Angeles, CA Willard Gates 513–555–3456
By:	J. S. Sebastian
Date:	11/5/—

EQUIPMENT INVENTORY. *This information is vital for proper engineering design. When the specifications of new equipment are unknown, the engineers may work with a worst-case scenario in designing engineering systems.*

reupholstering or other refinishing. This may require drawings and specifications similar to those prepared for new furnishings. Files and other metal furniture may be repainted electrostatically on-site. Other furniture, however, may have to be taken to a shop for work and temporary furniture may have to be provided for employee use during that period.

Equipment presents different problems. Office equipment is almost always specified and purchased by the client. Its characteristics, however, have a profound effect on the design of the office space, particularly the engineering systems.

The most useful source of information regarding equipment is obtained from manufacturer's specification sheets, which are usually readily available from dealers or from the manufacturers themselves. When these *cut sheets* are not available, as may be the case with older equipment, a physical inventory must be done by tape measure and examination of the name plate attached to the equipment.

As with furniture, an inventory catalog page may be prepared with a code, description, manufacturer's name, and model number for each unique piece. Technical information required by the design team and engineers includes size, weight, and required clearances and mechanical, electrical, communications, and plumbing requirements. A summary sheet with quantities and locations may also be prepared.

CARPET

Carpet is the almost universally accepted floor finish material for offices, exceptions being resilient flooring for workrooms and storage areas, ceramic tile for toilet rooms and food service kitchens, and wood or stone flooring as a decorative embellishment for high-design areas.

Carpet is used for its attractive appearance, its feel and resiliency underfoot, and for its acoustic value. It is the sound absorbent characteristics of carpet that make modern open planning practical. Carpet is reasonably priced, durable enough to last the life of most leases, and relatively easy to maintain.

Traffic, appearance, and cost are primary determinants in the selection of carpeting. Lobbies, dining rooms, assembly areas, and public corridors will generally get the most abuse and require the hardest-wearing carpeting. At the other end of the scale are executive areas where traffic is light and appearance is the primary selection criteria. In the middle are general office areas where most good quality commercial carpets will prove satisfactory and cost may become the determining factor.

The characteristics of carpeting to be considered by architects and interior designers in the selection of carpeting include fiber, construction, quantitative specifications, texture, coloration, underpad and installation method.

Carpet Fiber

The most popular and most natural carpet fiber was wool. For office projects, wool has largely been replaced by nylon except in specialized executive areas. Other carpet fibers are acrylic, olefin, and polyester. Different fibers are often blended in the finished carpet to take advantage of the best characteristics of each.

❏ Wool is the quality standard against which other carpet fibers are judged. Its biggest drawback is cost, which may restrict its use to selected high design areas. Wool is colorfast, flexible, durable, naturally flame resistant, and soil resistant.

❏ Nylon is the most common commercial carpet fiber, installed in the vast majority of office projects. It is the strongest, lightest, longest-wearing, and most abrasion resistant of all synthetic fibers. It is easily cleaned. Its major disadvantage is the build-up of static electricity, which must be overcome by special construction of the carpet.

❏ Acrylic carpet is the most similar to wool in appearance and feel. It takes dyes well and is resistant to sunlight and moisture. It produces the least static electricity of any carpet material. Although colorfast, acrylic carpets tend to fade and lose their life after cleaning.

❏ Olefin or polypropylene is strong, durable, and abrasion resistant. It resists stains, fading, and chemicals. However, it lacks resiliency and texture retention and softens at relatively low temperatures and is thus susceptible to searing from the hot seaming iron during installation.

❏ Polyester fibers are durable and take color well. Unless constructed with static control yarn, static electricity can be a problem. Polyester fiber melts at relatively low temperatures.

Carpet Construction

Carpets may be constructed by knitting or felting and Oriental rugs by handknotting, but the most common construction methods for commercial carpeting are weaving and tufting. Woven carpet is the traditional method of commercial carpet production but, because of cost, has largely been replaced by tufting except for special high traffic or high design areas.

❏ Woven carpets include Wiltons, Axminsters, and velvets, which differ in the complexity of weaving method. Because the face fiber and backing are interlocked in the weaving process, woven carpets are dimensionally stable and very hard wearing. Velvet is the most common but is suitable only for solid colors. Wiltons and Axminsters are often used in the public areas of hotels where the combination of very heavy wear resistance and bold patterns and colors are desired.

❏ Tufted carpet is far less expensive than woven carpet and constitutes the majority of the carpet produced. It is produced by stitching the face yarn through the fabric backing, creating a loop or *tuft*, much like a sewing machine stitches thread into a piece of cloth. Latex is often used to bond the tufts to the backing material. Often a urethane foam backing is applied when the carpet will be installed without separate padding. A variation of tufting is fusion bonding, in which the yarn piles are embedded in liquid vinyl. This results in exceptional tuft-binding strength.

Carpet backing materials may be of jute or synthetic material. Jute is dimensionally stable and heat resistant. Its drawback is its tendency to shrink or stain the face fibers when wet. Polypropylene is the most common synthetic backing material. While resistant to wetness, it is too sensitive to heat for hot-melt tape seaming and can unravel or fray when cut.

Quantitative Specifications

Carpet quality is determined by its characteristics of yarn weight and construction, pile height, face weight, total weight, and stitching density. It is these characteristics in combination that determine the wearability of the carpet. A heavy, dense carpet will withstand more abuse than a lighter carpet of the same fiber and construction; it will also cost more. For large projects, quantitative specifications can often be adjusted to produce special carpets precisely matched to the needs of the project.

❏ Yarn count and denier are measures of the coarseness of fiber strands, heavier deniers generally offering more strength, resiliency, and abrasion resistance. Strands may be twisted together to create yarn. *Two-ply* or *four-ply* are terms indicating the number of strands in the yarn. Light twisting gives a velvet texture to cut pile carpet. Tight twisting produces a nubby or frieze effect. If the strands used to make up the plies are of different colors, a heather effect is produced.

❏ Face weight is the weight of pile fiber per square yard of carpet. Total weight is the weight of pile fiber plus backing per square yard of carpet. Generally, the heavier the weight, the greater the resistance to wear and abuse.

❏ Pile height is the height of pile fiber above the backing. Total thickness is pile height plus the thickness of the backing. A thicker carpet may be more luxurious but makes maneuverability of wheelchairs and chairs with casters more difficult. Accessibility standards may limit pile height to a maximum of one-half inch.

❏ Stitching density is the number of stitches per unit area of carpet and is measured in a number of ways. Gauge is the measure of the distance between rows across the width of tufted carpet. A 1/8" gauge indicates that there are eight rows of tufts per inch. Stitches per inch measures stitches in the longitudinal direction. For woven carpets, pitch measures the number of rows in a 27" width of carpet, so must be divided by 27 to allow a direct comparison with the gauge of tufted carpet. In woven carpets, rows per inch is equivalent to the stitches per inch in tufted carpet.

Carpet Texture

Carpets are available in a variety of surface patterns or textures. These are created by either leaving the yarn loops as woven or tufted, called loop pile, or by cutting the loops resulting in a cut pile. Loop pile and cut pile can be combined to create many different surface textures.

Level loop pile carpet makes a smooth, level surface with excellent wear resistance. Multi-level loop pile carpet is made up of loops of different heights, giving a sculptured effect.

Cut pile carpet has a luxurious look that varies from smooth to nubby depending on the twist in the yarns used. Cut pile carpeting shows directional shading depending on how light hits the pile. This is considered an attractive feature of cut pile carpet, but unless specifically pointed out to clients, it may be thought to be a defect.

Coloration

The color, luster, and relative lightness or darkness of carpeting is a matter of aesthetics but also of resistance to soiling. A carpet that is too dark may show dusty footprints; a carpet that is too light will show dark dirt. Multi-colored carpets show soil less than solid colored. High luster may be aesthetically objectionable and tends to soil easily. Appearance is also affected by colorfastness and the resistance to fading from sunlight.

Carpets receive their color naturally or by dying. Natural wool carpeting is available in a variety of whites, browns, and blacks and may also be dyed. Synthetic fibers may be solution dyed with color added before the polymer is extruded, yarn dyed, or piece dyed. Patterns and colors may also be printed on finished carpeting.

Carpet manufacturers make available

a wide range of standard colors and will generally provide special colors if minimum yardage requirements are met. Even standard colors, however, may show slight but noticeable color variations between dye lots, and all carpet in a given project should be specified to be from the same dye lot.

Underpadding

Carpet underpads or cushions can add years to the life of a carpet. They are made of natural hair or fiber or of sponge rubber or urethane foam. Natural hair or fiber underpads are generally mothproof, sterile, and noncombustible. However, they can mildew if they get wet. Synthetic underpads resist moisture but may be susceptible to heat or burning.

Installation

Basic carpet types include wall-to-wall broadloom, carpet tiles, and area rugs. Wall-to-wall broadloom installation may be either glued down or stretched over padding. Carpet tiles are a necessity with raised access flooring and flat cable wiring installations. Area rugs, such as Orientals, may be used over wood or stone flooring.

❏ When carpet is installed stretched over padding, the first step is the placement of pieces of wood studded with nails known as *tackless strips* around the perimeter of the space. The underpad is glued to the floor within the tackless stripping. The carpet is then stretched taut and anchored to the nail points of the tackless stripping. Where widths of carpet meet in the middle of the floor, they are joined by tape with a glue that, when heated, joins the pieces together. Traditionally pieces of carpet were sewn together, but this has been replaced by heat-taping because of cost.

❏ Glue-down application is recommended for high traffic areas. The substrate must be cleaned well and the glue spread evenly. The carpet is laid and then rolled to insure even adhesion.

❏ Carpet tiles, generally 18" to 24" square, are generally installed loose, occasionally lightly glued to insure stability. When good quality carpet tiles are laid with the texture running in the same direction, the joints between tile may virtually disappear. Checkerboard and other patterns may also be created. Carpet tiles must be used over raised access flooring and when flat cable wiring is used. Carpet tiles also have long-term maintenance advantages. Tiles showing wear in high traffic areas may be easily replaced or switched with other tiles.

Other Considerations

Carpets must meet building codes for flammability. Indoor air pollution may result due to the off-gassing of chemicals used in carpet manufacture. Static electricity, while annoying to humans, can be deadly for computers. Special construction may be required, particularly for nylon carpets, to bring static electricity within acceptable limits.

RESILIENT FLOORING AND BASE

Resilient flooring is used for operational office areas where an inexpensive, easily cleaned, durable surface is required and acoustical considerations are unimportant. Typical uses are in file rooms and work rooms. Resilient flooring is the finish material on raised access flooring when carpet tiles are not used.

Common resilient flooring materials used in the past include linoleum, asphalt tile, and vinyl asbestos tile. Today they have been largely replaced by vinyl, vinyl composition, cork, and rubber. These materials vary in resilience, durability, and resistance to moisture and chemicals. Some resilient flooring is available with foam backing, making it softer underfoot.

Resilient flooring comes in a wide variety of colors, patterns and, sometimes, textures. When laid with pattern lines running parallel, the tile joints for some patterns virtually disappear. Solid colors tend to show dirt and scuff marks. Resilient flooring also comes in simulated brick, stone, and wood patterns that may be objectionable on aesthetic grounds.

Resilient flooring is available as tile, usually 9" by 9" or 12" by 12", or as sheet flooring. Thickness is usually less than 1/4". Resilient flooring is set in mastic.

Rubber or vinyl base, usually either 2½" or 4" high, is used to protect finished walls from damage. Straight base is used with carpet and coved base with resilient flooring. Base is available in a variety of solid colors with dark brown or black being the most widely used.

WINDOW COVERINGS

In buildings for lease, window coverings are usually specified and installed by the landlord. To maintain the exterior appearance of the building, substitutions are rarely allowed for window coverings. To achieve wide acceptance, landlords generally select an off-white neutral color. When decorative curtains or draperies are desired or when black-out shades, linings, or draperies are needed, these are usually installed by the tenant on the inside of the building standard window covering.

The primary function of window coverings is the control of exterior light, particularly glare, and the reduction of heat loads from the exterior. To achieve optimum results, the amount of *sheer*, or light allowed to pass through the window covering, must be carefully calculated and controlled. Curtains and draperies also absorb sound and affect the acoustic characteristics of a space.

Common window coverings are curtains or draperies and vertical or horizontal mini-blinds. Horizontal mini-blinds are made of metal in a variety of finishes and may be perforated for glare control. Materials for curtains and draperies are closely regulated by building codes. As loose, hanging fabrics, curtains and draperies in commercial use generally must be incombustible.

CHAPTER ELEVEN

CONTRACT DOCUMENTS

Good design requires good implementation. A poorly detailed or poorly constructed project can jeopardize the best design intentions. Good execution begins with contract documents.

Construction and *furnishings* documents consist of the drawings and specifications issued to the contractors, vendors, and installers for the purpose of building and furnishing the office project. They are based on *design development* documents approved by the client and, in some cases, *scope* documents approved by the landlord. Contract documentation is the most time-consuming phase of the professional service contact, generally accounting for 30 to 40 percent of the total basic service fee.

Additional staff are often required to assist in the production of the working drawings. With the project team at its maximum size, conscientious organization is needed. A schedule with time and work allocations for each individual should be developed, and in-house job meetings should be held frequently to review assignments and progress.

Base building drawings and specifications need to be reviewed as a basis for interiors construction and furnishings documents. Floor plan backgrounds prepared for the design phases of the project should again be checked against base building drawings and field conditions.

Sheet sizes, layouts, and drawing scales need to be determined. Unusual scales should be avoided as they may be visually misinterpreted by contractors and others. Sheet sizes should be selected to match standards used by the CADD plotter and the printing company. Borders are helpful to indicate to the printer the limit of the drawing and as cutting and binding guidelines.

Standard conventions, symbols, and abbreviations need to be determined. Sometimes landlords issue guidelines for drawings and insist on certain drafting conventions being followed. This may extend to sheet numbering, column identification, and symbol standardization.

A schedule of regular in-house reviews should be established. Sets of record prints should be produced, usually weekly, to be used for checking and as a record of work produced in case of contract disagreements. Some firms have a program for quality assurance that includes periodic review of documents by nonteam members and checklists for code compliance, detail accuracy and completeness, and graphic standards.

Protection of documents should be considered. Manually drafted originals may be protected with periodic reproducible mylar or sepia prints made as back-up in case of damage to the originals. Computer aided design and drafting (CADD) data may be protected by periodic duplication on tape or disks that are then stored in a remote location.

CONSTRUCTION AND FURNISHINGS DRAWINGS

Working drawings show contractors what is to be constructed or furnished. They may be produced manually or on a CADD system.

CADD is now an accepted standard method for producing contract documents. It has many advantages. If space planning or design has been done on CADD, construction documents are a continuation of the process; redrawing is not necessary. CADD is potentially more accurate; small-scale drawings can be enlarged electronically for detailing. It can be tied to a data base and used to produce budgets, schedules, and specifications of furnishings and construction items. CADD can be used for ongoing facility management to track personnel, telephones, square footage, furniture components, and a myriad of other information.

A basic concept of CADD is that information is developed and stored in layers. A project may consist of dozens or hundreds of layers stored in the computer, each containing a specific type of information. These layers are then combined to produce finished drawings. For example, a floor plan background layer may be combined with an electrical outlet layer and a telephone outlet layer to produce an outlet plan. These, in turn, may be combined with a furniture layer for coordination. If an item must be revised the change is made only once to the appropriate layer.

With manual drafting the scale of a drawing must be determined ahead of time. Plan blow-ups must be separately drawn. With CADD all drawings are created "full size"; the concept of scale is only introduced for the plotting and printing process. Producing drawings at any scale, showing any degree of detail, is a matter of selecting the appropriate scale to be plotted. Plan drawings are most commonly produced at a scale of 1/8" = 1'0". For very large projects, 1/16" = 1'0" may be used, although enlarged plans of complex areas may be necessary. For smaller projects, 1/4" = 1'0" is another common scale and may permit drawings that are normally drawn separately, such as the construction plan and the outlet plan, to be combined.

As a general principle, dimensions, notes, and other indications should never be duplicated from drawing to drawing. Dimensions shown on the construction plan should not also be shown on elevations, for example. Ideally this will reduce drawing time, ambiguity, and errors. Like all rules, however, if carried to extremes, the result may be confusion. If a contractor must refer to five or six sheets of drawings in order to fully understand a given item, the rule has probably been carried too far. Construction documents are a means of communication between the architect or interior designer and the contractors; the overriding principle is that they be as clear as possible.

Demolition Plan

The demolition plan is used when existing space is to be remodeled. Before the demolition plan is prepared, a survey of the existing space should be conducted. This survey should be accurate, although it does not need to be as precise as a measured drawing of construction intended to remain. The demolition plan should show an outline of the physical limits of the work on the floor. All existing construction should be shown. Items to remain are indicted by solid lines, while items to be removed are usually shown with dotted lines and may include partitions, doors, floor coverings, window coverings, cabinetwork, lighting, ceilings, and outlets. Notes should clarify any areas of confusion.

Construction Plan

The construction plan is actually a section drawing drawn at a height of approximately four feet above the floor. It shows all partitions, doors, cabinetwork, and other general construction work on the project. Partition types may be shown by cross-hatching, the hatching pattern indicating whether the partition is standard interior, demountable, acoustical, fire rated, or some other configuration. Existing partitions, both core and shell and office interior, are usually shown unhatched.

The physical boundaries of the work should be shown. Core areas are often shaded or cross-hatched to indicate that they are outside the scope of office interior construction work.

Dimensioning on the construction plan usually begins with a fixed reference point, such as the structural column grid. New construction is located with reference to this grid. Drywall partitions are usually dimensioned to the centerline of the stud. This makes the partitions easy to relate to a modular pattern of column centerlines, exterior window mullions, ceiling tiles, or light fixtures. Where criti-

cal dimensions must be maintained for recesses for filing cabinets, dimensions (identified as *clear*) may be shown to the face of a finished wall. Where new partitions must be flush with existing construction, arrows labeled *align* may be used.

The conventional symbol for a door with frame and hardware on a construction plan is a hexagon. There are two distinct methods of identifying and scheduling doors. In the traditional architectural method, each opening is assigned a unique, consecutive number. A schedule matrix is prepared with columns for the characteristics of size, door material and finish, frame type, hardware, and so forth. Each opening is then listed and defined in numerical order. This door schedule can be a lengthy document since each specification may be repeated many times.

A second method is to identify each opening by type, indicated by a single letter or number, or a combination of three letter/numbers used to indicate, respectively, door type, frame type, and hardware set. A door schedule is prepared by opening type. The contractor is responsible for determining the quantity of each type. This method is appropriate for interior office construction where there are usually many identical openings.

There are design implications in the choice of door schedule methodology. By treating each opening uniquely, the traditional door schedule emphasizes differences; each opening is a separate line item and relationships between openings are irrelevant. The door type method, on the other hand, encourages a search for similarities and the development of modular systems.

Door swings should be shown in their fully open position—this is a drafting convention that helps in the location of

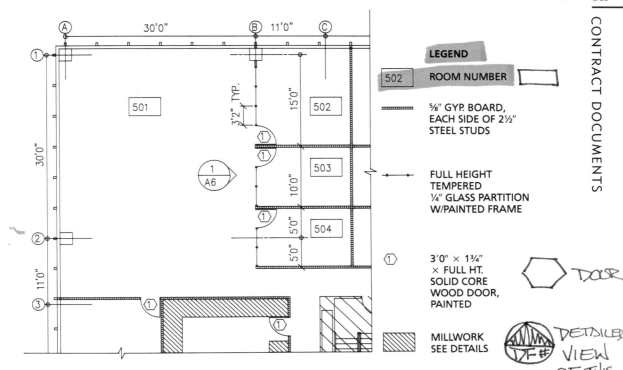

CONSTRUCTION PLAN. *The construction plan shows the location and construction of partitions and doors, locates architectural woodwork, and gives reference notations for room numbers, elevations, and details.*

light switches and other devices and helps to prevent door swings from interfering with furniture, cabinetwork, or light fixtures.

Doors in the corners of rooms are usually not dimensioned. Contractors will automatically locate the door jamb approximately four to six inches from the intersecting partition. If a more precise dimension is important to the design concept, it should be indicated.

The construction plan is the basic reference drawing for the set of construction documents. It should include room names and numbers and elevation and detail references. At a point in the drawing's preparation, when all partitions and doors have been drawn but not cross-hatched or dimensioned, reproducible prints should be made to serve as backgrounds for all other plan drawings. This is necessary when drawings are prepared manually; on CADD, this background will simply be another layer in the system.

Ceiling Plan

The ceiling plan shows the ceiling, light fixtures, sprinkler heads, and visible HVAC devices. Unlike other plan drawings, the ceiling plan is not a real view looking down at the floor. It is the view one would see looking down if the floor were mirrored and is thus usually called a *reflected ceiling plan.*

The ceiling plan duplicates the visible elements of the electrical engineer's light-

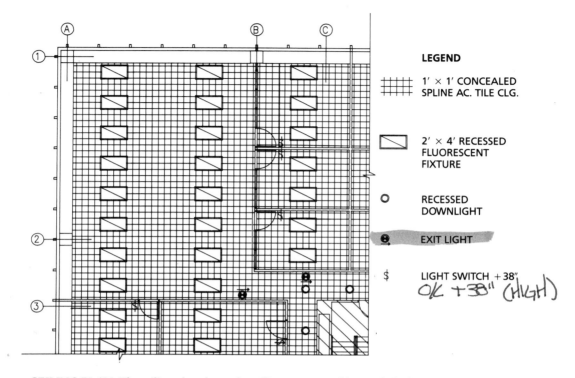

LEGEND

1' × 1' CONCEALED
SPLINE AC. TILE CLG.

2' × 4' RECESSED
FLUORESCENT
FIXTURE

RECESSED
DOWNLIGHT

EXIT LIGHT

LIGHT SWITCH + 38"
OK + 38" (HIGH)

CEILING PLAN. The ceiling plan shows the ceiling pattern and locates light fixtures and sprinklers (not shown in this example).

ing plan, the mechanical engineer's HVAC plan, and the plumbing engineer's sprinkler layout. Whereas the engineering drawings are concerned with circuiting, ductwork, and piping, the ceiling plan of the architect or interior designer is concerned with location, appearance, and spatial relationships. Contractors are directed to refer to the ceiling plan for the location of ceiling elements and to the engineering drawings for technical operational details.

The acoustical tile pattern is generally fully drawn on the ceiling plan. If the full ceiling is to be installed before the partitions, a single start point for the overall tile pattern, usually related to the column grid, is shown. If the ceiling is to be installed on a room-by-room basis after the partitions have been installed, start points for the tile pattern in each area must be identified, although for rectangular rooms a general note to the effect that the perimeter row of tile should not be less than half a tile in width may be sufficient.

The ceiling plan should show drywall and plaster ceilings and soffits with detail references. It should show the location of all light fixtures including exit and emergency lighting, fire protection sprinklers and warning devices, and HVAC grilles and diffusers. It is usually not necessary to dimension these items except in critical situations; counting tiles is usually sufficient for determining a precise

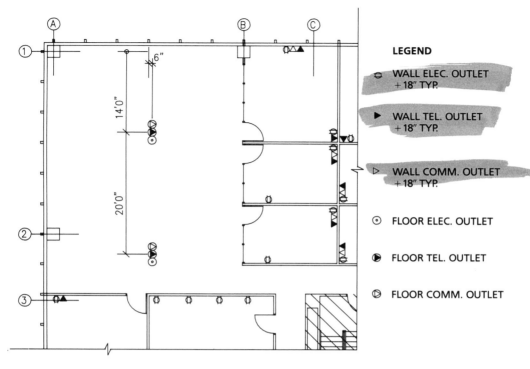

OUTLET PLAN. The outlet plan locates electrical and communications outlets. Circuiting is usually shown on engineering drawings. In this example, electrified open plan workstation panels are fed through floor outlets. Furniture may be shown dotted for reference.

location. Although located on partitions, light switches are often shown on the ceiling plan for convenience.

Outlet Plan

The outlet plan shows the location of electrical and communications outlets in the project. Like the ceiling plan, this drawing duplicates information found on the electrical engineer's power and communication plan and the drawings of the telephone or computer installer. The contractor uses the architect's or interior designer's outlet plan for location and the engineering drawings for circuiting.

Wall outlets are shown to be located at a standard height unless indicated otherwise. Care should be taken to avoid back-to-back outlets for acoustical reasons and to specify outlet heights in accordance with requirements for the disabled.

Floor outlets are shown and dimensioned from partitions or the column grid. If there is an underfloor ductwork system, this should be shown. Outlets should be coordinated with furniture, and for that reason, furniture is often shown on the outlet plan for reference. A dimensional tolerance of several inches usually must be allowed in locating floor outlets. If coordination with open plan workstations is critical, contractors may be directed to lay out both furniture and outlets on the bare floor for review by the architect or interior designer before construction begins.

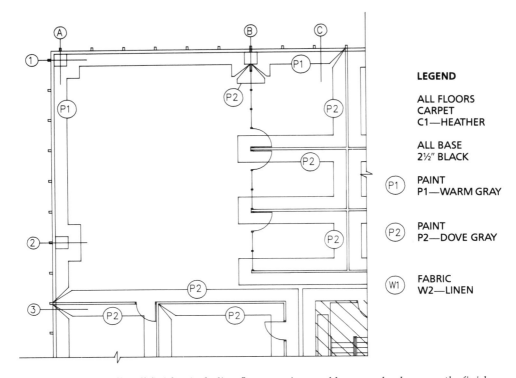

FINISH PLAN. All wall finishes including floor coverings and base may be shown on the finishes plan. If the plan becomes too crowded, a separate floor finishes plan may be required.

Finish Plan/Floor Finish Plan

The finish plan shows the finish material to be applied to wall and floor surfaces. Traditionally this information was shown on a finish schedule, which is a matrix showing each room by number with columns for each wall surface, floor, base, and wainscoting or other special features. For interior office projects, this schedule is usually replaced with a finish plan that has graphic clarity and is less error-prone.

The finish plan graphically brackets and codes each finished surface and keys it to a legend and specification. The code may indicate a single wall finish or a combination of trim, wall surface, wainscot, and base. If trim or base finish is the same throughout, a general note may be sufficient. If the majority of walls have the same finish, this may also be indicated in a note. Brackets on the drawing would then indicate only exceptions.

In drawing the brackets, door openings are usually ignored to insure that surfaces above doors, in corners, or between paired doors do not get ignored. Finishes on doors and frames are usually specified in a note or on the door schedule.

On most projects floor finishes and wall finishes can be indicated on one drawing. Where the floor pattern is complex, a separate floor finish drawing may be desirable.

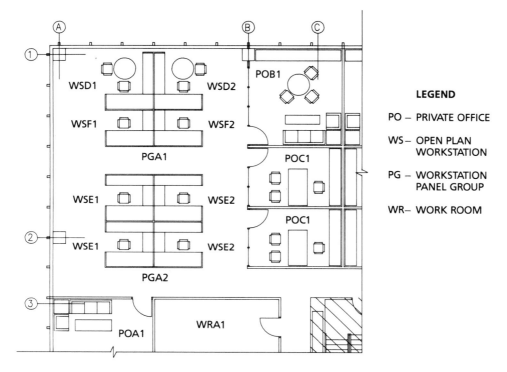

LEGEND

PO – PRIVATE OFFICE

WS– OPEN PLAN
WORKSTATION

PG – WORKSTATION
PANEL GROUP

WR– WORK ROOM

FURNISHINGS PLAN. In this example each room and workstation is given a workplace designation, as is the panel grouping in each open plan workstation cluster. Components within each workplace are then listed on a workplace catalog page and described in detail in a component specification.

Furniture Plan

The furniture plan shows each piece of loose furniture, drawn to scale. Furniture is usually not located by dimension except for open plan workstation systems. A primary purpose of the furniture plan from the furniture dealer's point of view is that it can be used to locate and count the number of each specific furniture type.

On relatively simple projects each individual piece of furniture and each open plan workstation component may be coded and keyed to a furniture schedule in the specifications. On more complex projects, another layer of organization may be used to improve clarity. Each workplace, including each open plan workstation and panel cluster, may be coded as a unit and keyed to a workplace catalog and component schedule in the specifications. This is explained in greater detail later in this chapter.

Elevations

Elevations of walls and cabinetwork, usually drawn at a scale of 1/4" = 1'0" or 1/2" = 1'0", are drawn on the elevation drawings. The primary purpose of elevation drawings is for reference: to provide a graphic picture and to locate key details. Elevations are generally only drawn for walls that contain something interesting; there is usually no need to draw flat, unarticulated walls or walls that contain only standard doors.

Usually only vertical dimensions are shown on elevation drawings; horizontal dimensions are shown on floor plans. Wall finishes should be indicated with codes relating to the finish plan.

Details

Details take many forms and are drawn at many different scales. For clarity, an effort should be made to keep the scale the same for all drawings on any one sheet. Details should be dimensionally tied to column grids or reference points on the construction plan or elevations.

Details show the connections between materials. They should be as complete as possible and fully describe every condition on the project. Any condition not drawn should be unambiguously inferred from similar details.

Many architecture and interior design firms keep libraries of successful details either stored in the CADD system or in reference notebooks. Simple standard details showing standard installation methods may be used without revision; details with any complexity or that show connections to base building construction will usually have to be edited. There are also reference sources such as *Architectural Graphics Standards*, *Timesaver Standards*, and *Interior Graphic and Design Standards*, which are useful guides for detailing.

Engineering Drawings

Construction documents normally include drawings prepared by mechanical engineers for HVAC, plumbing, and sprinkler work, by electrical engineers for lighting and electrical power distribution, and, if necessary, by structural engineers for floor penetrations and reinforcement.

Engineering drawings are produced on floor plan backgrounds supplied by the architect or interior designer. If the engineering firm uses CADD, ideally it should be compatible with the system used by the design firm so that backgrounds and revision information can be exchanged electronically. Engineering check sets should be produced periodically and coordinated by the architect or interior designer.

SPECIFICATIONS

Specifications are written requirements for the materials and systems on the project and the level of quality and the standards to be met in the performance of the work. They accompany the contract drawings and have equal contractual weight.

Specifications are usually produced by word processor on 8½-by-11-inch paper and issued as a bound volume. On very small projects, specifications may be printed directly on the drawings.

Specifications are usually organized in packages depending on how the project will be bid and implemented. If construction, carpeting, and furniture are to be the three major prime contractors on the project, each will have a separate specification package.

Specifications are commonly organized according to the masterformat of the Construction Specification Institute (CSI). This format assigns all trades, products, and services to one of sixteen divisions. *Sweet's Catalog*, the standard reference for construction materials and products, follows this arrangement. This system allows architects, interior designers, contractors, and suppliers to know immediately and with confidence where to look in a specification for a particular item.

Division 1 of the specifications presents "General Requirements," which describes the administrative and procedural requirements for the project. Items that may be included are the contractors' responsibilities for schedules and job meetings, shop drawing submittals, substitution procedures, coordination with the landlord and other prime contractors, punch list procedures, and clean-up.

Divisions 2 through 16 are materials or trade divisions. Specification divisions of particular relevance to interior construction and furnishings include division 6, "Wood and Plastic," which includes architectural woodwork; division 8, "Doors and Windows"; division 9, "Finishes," which includes drywall partitioning, acoustical ceilings, floor finishes, paint, and wall coverings; division 10, "Specialties," which includes demountable partitions and raised access flooring; and division 12, "Furnishings." The engineers on the project will prepare specifications for division 15, "Mechanical," and division 16, "Electrical."

Within each division, each trade, material, or system is organized by section. For example, section 06400 is "Architectural Woodwork," section 09680 is "Carpet," and section 12600 is "Furniture and Accessories."

Each specification section consists of three parts. The first is "General Requirements," which includes the scope of the work, the work not included, references to published standards, submittal requirements, quality assurance measures, site conditions, delivery, storage, and handling procedures.

The second part is "Products," which includes a listing of materials, manufacturers, equipment, and components covered in the specification section. The third part is "Execution," which details the procedures for preparation, construction, installation, testing, and field quality control of the item.

As a general principle, specifications should describe the results expected and avoid telling the contractor how such results are to be achieved. While this is not always practical, the primary responsibility of the contractor for means, methods, and procedures should be respected.

Several approaches are used in preparing specifications. The first is *performance specifying*. In a performance specification, the end result is defined in great detail without mentioning brand names or particular products. A performance specification for carpeting, for example, will list type of weave, surface texture, gauge, face weight, backing materials, and so on—all the qualities required in the product.

Proprietary specifications, on the other hand, list one or more acceptable products by brand name, model, or pattern. Instead of listing detailed requirements for carpeting, for example, one need only state the name of the mill and the selected pattern.

Performance specifications are most appropriate for generic materials, such as woodwork and drywall, where many manufacturers supply comparable products and mill or jobsite fabrication is the primary consideration. They allow anyone who can meet the detailed requirements to bid on the project and thus encourage the greatest competition and, ideally, the lowest price. Performance specifications are commonly required for government projects. Performance specifications are generally longer, more difficult to write, and require a deeper technical knowledge on the part of the architect or interior designer.

Performance specifications often refer to national standards published by industry associations and testing organizations. Standards are published by the American Society for Testing and Materials (ASTM), American National Standards Institute (ANSI), the Architectural

Woodwork Institute (AWI), the Tile Council, and many others. Specifiers should be sure they have read and understood a reference before including it in a specification.

Proprietary specifications are most appropriate for manufactured products where a unique design or appearance is required, such as furniture and light fixtures. For items such as these, performance specification is usually impractical. If bidding competition is required, several acceptable alternative products are listed.

A compromise between performance and proprietary specifications is to list several product names and then the words "or equal." This allows anyone to bid who can prove that his or her product is equivalent to the one specified.

There is risk involved. An "or equal" clause indicates that the design professional and client will consider any product in good faith. If an unacceptable product is offered, the architect or interior designer must take the time to prove, based on data submitted by the bidder, that the product is *not* an equal to that specified, sometimes a difficult task.

The AIA and CSI both publish master specifications that can be purchased and then edited for use on projects. Even if not rigorously followed, master specifications are helpful as a start to specification writing and as a check against omissions. Master specifications are available on computer disks.

For office interiors projects the longest and most complex specification is generally division 12, "Furnishings," particularly when open plan workstations are involved. To provide clarity, a hierarchy of organization may help to order the project. At the top of the hierarchy may be the furniture plan, then the workplace catalog, and finally the specification of the components making up the workplace.

This organization may begin at the furniture plan. Instead of identifying every piece of furniture and component on the plan, each workplace may be designated by code. This code may relate to the space program (A, B, C, etc.), indicating size and/or job function of the workplace. To indicate variations within each general workplace type, a suffix may be used (A1, A2, A3, etc.). As a reminder about the general type of workplace, prefixes such as WS for open plan workstations or PO for private office may be added so that the code shown on the furniture plan may take the form WSA1, WSA2, POB3, and so forth.

The next level of organization is the workplace catalog. This consists of a separate page for each specific workplace that contains a listing of its furniture and components. Each piece of furniture and component is coded and identified. As an aid to visualization, the page may include a plan or isometric drawing of the workplace.

A complication to this process is the method used to account for shared panels between workstations in an open plan workstation cluster. If panels are provided as shown on each workstation drawing, panels shared between two workstations will obviously be ordered twice. One method used to avoid this is not to include panels in the component list in the workstation catalog but to develop a separate catalog page for each panel cluster configuration.

The third and final step in the hierarchy is the component specification. This is a list of every piece of furniture and component shown in the workstation catalog and includes a description by manufacturer, model number, size, finish, and special features such as locks.

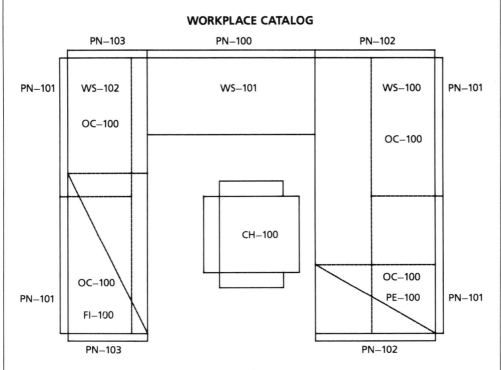

WORKPLACE CATALOG

| PROJECT: | Tyrell Corporation/Operations Center |
| WORKPLACE: | WSE3/Research Analyst |

Code	Quantity	Description
WS–100	1	Primary worksurface 72"w × 30"d
WS–101	1	Return 42"w × 20"d
WS–102	1	Credenza worksurface 72"w × 20"d
PE–100	1	Pedestal 18"w × 30"d w/2 box drawers, legal file drawer, locks
FI–100	1	2 drawer lateral file 40"w × 18"d
OC–100	4	Overhead storage cabinet 36"w × 16"d, flipper door, lock
PN–100	1	Panel, 42"w × 60"h
PN–101	4	Panel, 36"w × 60"h
PN–102	2	Panel, 30"w × 60"h
PN–103	2	Panel, 20"w × 18"h
CH–100	1	Desk chair

| Date: | 11/5/— |

WORKPLACE CATALOG. *A separate page is prepared for each workplace configuration on the project. If the panels in this example were part of a cluster and identified as a separate workplace, they would be shown with a dotted line and not listed here.*

COMPONENT SPECIFICATIONS

Code	Description	Finish
WS-100	Primary worksurface Tredway # NU1–J7230PL 72"w × 30"d	Plastic laminate gray 840
WS-101	Return Tredway # NU1–K4220PL 42"w × 20"d	Plastic laminate gray 840
WS-102	Credenza worksurface Tredway # NU1–J7220PL 72"w × 20"d	Plastic laminate gray 840
PE-100	Pedestal Tredway # JO3–1830ML 18"w × 30"d × 28"h 2 box drawers # FV367L 1 legal file drawer # FC456L with locks	Metal black 500
FI-100	Lateral file Tredway # FI2–4018ME 40"w × 18"d × 28"h 2 drawers # GH232L with locks	Metal black 500
OC-100	Overhead storage cabinet Tredway # OB6–3616ML 36"w × 16"d × 14"h cabinet with flipper door	Metal black 500
PN-100	Workstation panel Tredway # PQ3–4260AF–E 42"w × 2"d × 60"h electrified base	Fabric Pinwool gray 556
PN-101	Workstation panel Tredway # PQ3–3660AF 36"w × 2"d × 60"h standard base	Fabric Pinwool gray 556

COMPONENT SPECIFICATIONS. *This documents the complete specification for each piece of furniture and furniture component on the project and is used by the furniture contractor to develop unit prices.*

GENERAL AND SUPPLEMENTARY CONDITIONS

A third major component of contract documents are the general and supplementary conditions. General conditions are the basic legal rights and responsibilities of the parties to the contract. They are the same for most projects and are standardized. Frequently used general conditions are the AIA document A201, "General Conditions of the Contract for Construction," and AIA and ASID documents A271, "General Conditions of the Contract for Furniture, Furnishings, and Equipment." When used, these are included without annotations in the contract.

When general conditions must be modified, supplementary conditions are written. Supplementary conditions are revisions to the general conditions applicable to the particular project. In format, supplementary conditions refer directly to paragraphs in the general conditions and state the exact additions, revisions, or deletions.

The decision about which items should be covered in contract conditions and which in specification sections is often arbitrary. As a general rule, items should not be repeated unnecessarily. On small projects contract conditions may be combined with the specifications into one section. They may be included on the drawings. Sometimes contract conditions are simply included in the agreement itself as in AIA document A117, "Abbreviated Form of Agreement Between Owner and Contractor," for construction projects of limited scope and AIA and ASID document A177, "Abbreviated Form of Agreement Between Owner and Contractor for Furniture, Furnishings, and Equipment."

Some of the information that should be included in general and supplementary conditions includes:

❑ A definition of the contract documents, the contract, and the distinction between the *project*, which is the entire office installation and may include many separate contractors, and the *work* that is to be performed by the particular contractor under the contract in question.

❑ A description of the duties and responsibilities of the architect or interior designer. If AIA or ASID documents are used, they have the advantage of being consistent with other AIA and ASID documents including B171, the "Agreement for Interior Design Services." These duties may include acting as the owner's agent, reviewing installation at the job-site for consistency with the contract documents, reviewing shop drawings and other submittals, issuing certificates of payment, preparing change orders, and determining dates of substantial and final completion. Often some of these duties may be performed by a furniture project manager or the owner's in-house purchasing or facility management department. Such modification of responsibilities should be described in the supplementary conditions.

❑ A description of the duties and responsibilities of the owner. The owner in this case is defined as the party who is purchasing the construction or furniture, not to be confused with the landlord or owner of the premises. The owner's responsibilities include, among other things, the obligation to provide access to the site, temporary utilities, and vertical transportation. The owner has the right to stop work under certain conditions and may have the work performed by others if the contractor fails to perform.

❏ A description of the duties and responsibilities of the contractor. The contractor's duties generally include inspection and verification of site access and conditions, preparation and maintenance of schedules, compliance with government regulations, preparation of shop drawings and other submissions, and performance and supervision of the work. The general conditions also define the contractor's relationship with any subcontractors who may be used for the construction, fabrication, delivery, or installation of the work.

❏ The obligation of the contractor to insure that their employees are compatible with other trades on the project or working in the building, including construction trade unions. Any cost implications of this requirement should be clarified at the time of bidding.

❏ Implications of the Date of Substantial Completion. This is generally the date when the owner may occupy the premises and when title passes from the contractor to the owner. This transfer has legal and insurance implications that may be covered by provisions of the Uniform Commercial Code as well as the contract documents.

❏ Conditions for payment including retention, partial payment, final payment, changes in the work, and payments withheld.

❏ Obligations of the contractor with regard to safety at the jobsite.

❏ Requirements for insurance. These should be developed in consultation with the owner's insurance advisor and attorney. The landlord may also have insurance requirements that must be met.

APPROVAL

Like the program and design documents of the project, the contract documents should be approved by the client. Clients may be reluctant to do this, and architects and interior designers may hesitate to insist, because of the mass of technical detail involved and the feeling that contract documents have little new information beyond that which was approved in the design development phase. New information is generated, however, in the refinement and detail that goes into the production of contract documents. Architects and interior designers who do not take the time to conduct an in-depth review of contract documents with their clients may be leaving themselves liable for serious misunderstandings during construction.

IMPLEMENTATION OPTIONS

There are a variety of approaches to project construction and furnishing. Construction may be accomplished by a general contractor, a construction manager, or a landlord acting as project manager. Furnishings may be acquired from dealers providing full service, through separate contracts for supply and installation or through the services of a furniture project manager.

General Contractors

The traditional and often simplest method of implementing interior construction is by a general contract. Complete contract documents are issued to general contractors who then solicit bids from specialized trade subcontractors.

Under a *fixed price contract*, the contractor is responsible only for providing exactly what is contained in the contract documents. This imposes an obligation on the architect or interior designer to insure that documents are as complete and correct as possible, since any errors or extra work required of the contractor may result in additional costs to the client.

Under fixed price contracts, general contractors' profits are the difference between their costs and their bids. When bids are too low, when projects are mismanaged, or when subcontractor or supplier prices come in higher than expected, contractors lose money.

Another type of general contract is the negotiated *cost-plus contract*. One or more general contractors are interviewed and invited to submit proposals describing how they would implement the project and the fees and profit margins they expect. Contracts are awarded on the basis of estimated costs and fixed percentages or amounts for general conditions' costs, overhead, and profit. This approach may be appropriate for fast-track projects where construction must begin before documents are complete or with contractors who have a long-standing relationship with the client. A negotiated contract implies a higher level of trust and cooperation between contractor, client, and design professional than with a fixed price contract.

The general contractor is usually responsible for performing all construction work on the project. Sometimes in the interest of saving time or money, contracts are split between several prime contractors. In addition to a contract for general construction, separate prime contracts may be executed for floor coverings, architectural woodwork, HVAC work, or electrical work. This requires extra coordination on the part of the client, architect, or interior designer and often leads to the hiring of a separate construction manager.

Construction Management

A second method of implementing construction is by employing a construction manager. A construction manager may perform the same services as a general contractor but is paid a professional fee like an architect or interior designer. The professional fee arrangement theoretically removes the profit motive and thus the adversarial relationship that often occurs with contractors. Construction managers are selected like architects, interior designers, and engineers based on track record, references, a fee proposal, and the perceived ability to do the project.

Like a general contractor, a construction manager solicits prices from trade contractors. Rather than being hired by the general contractor, however, the trade contractors are issued separate contracts by the client with the construction manager designated as the client's agent for the administration and coordination of their work.

Construction managers usually provide services beyond those of a general contractor. As a professional consultant to the project, construction managers may be retained early in the process, sometimes even before the architect or interior designer. They may develop project budgets and schedules and assist in the administration of fast-track or phased projects where coordination is complex. They may perform value engineering services by recommending alternate systems and material for evaluation and may review contract documents in progress. They may recommend potential trade bidders, prepare bid packages, tabulate and evaluate bids, and make recommendations to the client for contract award.

Relationships between design firms and construction managers can be strained if their roles are not clearly defined in their respective professional service contracts and if there is not a positive effort toward cooperation. The retention of a construction manager seldom reduces the work of the architect or interior designer; more often it is increased. Consideration of construction manager recommendations, assisting in developing separate bid packages for subcontractors, and the additional coordination required as the team expands, while in the best interest of the project, may require extra time on the part of the design professional.

Construction management is most appropriate for large, complex, fast-track, or phased projects, that is, projects where unusual emphasis and capability in management of the construction process may be required. In practice, the line between general contractor and construction manager is blurred and there are innumerable shadings to the possible relationships with clients.

Landlord Project Management

In new buildings where much of the construction work is paid for under the lease workletter, the entire construction process may be managed by the landlord under the lease agreement. Work may be performed by the base building contractor, an on-site tenant construction contractor, or bid by the landlord to a list of selected general contractors.

Drawings and specifications are submitted by the architect or interior designer to the landlord in accordance with the lease. After consulting with contractors, the landlord prepares an estimate of costs for the client's approval. Payment is by invoice from the landlord.

Often the interior construction drawings and specifications technically become amendments to base building contract documents. General conditions and specifications sections for the interiors work may be written in the form of addenda to these documents and include only those sections or paragraphs that differ from requirements of the base building.

Management by the landlord using an on-site contractor has many advantages, particularly for the landlord. Standard construction materials may be bulk purchased and prestocked on the floor. The learning curve for new contractors may be eliminated and work is performed at a predictable quality level. Paperwork and management procedures may be streamlined. The work of many tenants in the building may be efficiently scheduled and coordinated and fast-track procedures may be more easily implemented. On the other hand, the client may lose control when the landlord assumes responsibility for the construction process. Costs of nonstandard construction can be significantly higher. When nonstandard construction makes up a significant portion of the project, tenants may want to reserve the right during lease negotiations to use an outside contractor.

Furnishings Acquisition

Traditionally, furniture dealers are responsible for management and installation of furnishings as well as the performance of the manufacturers who are their suppliers or subcontractors. The architect or interior designer prepares furniture plans and specifications for bid to furniture dealers. The dealers, in turn, obtain prices from the manufacturers of the specified items, add costs for shipping, receiving, warehousing, delivery, installation, management, overhead, and profit and submit bids to the client. Clients, with the assistance of their architects and interior designers, then award contracts to one or more dealers.

Where only one manufacturer is specified for an item of furniture, each dealer presumably receives the same price from the manufacturer and competes with other dealers on the basis of overhead and profit. If alternate manufacturers are allowed by the specifications for a given item, competition between manufacturers is encouraged. A further refinement is introduced by the concept of franchised dealers, who receive favorable pricing from certain manufacturers in return for stocking, display, promotion, or other concessions. This limits competition for franchised items. Where franchised items from different manufacturers are specified, this may result in several dealers on a project, each supplying its own franchised product.

On large projects the tasks of management, manufacture, and installation may be contracted separately. Instead of bidding to dealers, bids for "supply only" may be requested directly from manufacturers. Bids for "installation only" may be solicited from furniture dealers or specialized furniture installation contractors. Coordination and management may be provided by the manufacturer or installer for additional compensation or by a dealer, furniture consultant, or project manager who is retained on a professional service contract. This furniture project manager is analogous to the construction manager for general construction.

The duties of the furniture project manager may include budgeting and scheduling, preparation of detailed quantity schedules, purchase requisitions and final installation drawings, coordination of customer's own material (COM), monitoring manufacturing, arranging for transportation, warehousing and installation, supervision of installation, preparation of punch lists, and the processing of invoices and claims. Additionally the furniture project manager may manage the inventory of existing furnishings and implement repair and refurbishing.

BIDDING AND NEGOTIATION

The architect or interior designer is generally responsible for managing the bid or negotiation process on behalf of the client. This consists of qualifying bidders, preparing bid documents including clarifications and addenda during the bidding, and assisting the owner in the analysis of prices and the preparation of contracts.

On government projects all qualified parties who can meet the specifications and bonding requirements generally must be permitted to bid. On private work the owner has the right to pick and choose. The architect or interior designer generally prepares a list of bidders whom he or she believes to be qualified to perform the work. The client reviews, amends, and approves the list. Generally three to five bidders are sufficient to insure reasonable competition.

Qualifications for inclusion on a bid list might include previous working experience with the client, architect, or interior designer, references from other organizations who have used their services, and financial credentials. Contractors should be able to demonstrate integrity, management capability, construction and installation quality, and long-term service.

Bid Documents

Bid documents include the invitation and instructions to bidders, bid form, and contract documents. Some of the information that should be in the invitation and instructions to bidders includes:

❑ Date, time, and place bids will be received. Bidders should be informed that no bids will be accepted after the time stated and that no verbal or telephoned bids or qualifications will be considered.

❏ Whether the bid opening will be public or private. On government projects bid openings generally must be public. For private clients many architects and interior designers recommend private bid openings as a matter of policy. Bids are often so complicated that conclusions reached without thorough analysis may be incorrect and public bid openings can lead to misunderstandings. Consideration should also be given to the fact that owners on private projects are not obligated to accept the lowest bid. While award to the low bidder is not required, all things being equal, the low bidder generally receives the contract.

❏ Procedures for addenda and clarifications. The architect or interior designer should make sure that all information given to bidders during the bid period be in writing and be distributed to all bidders. This includes answers to bidders' questions, requests for substitutions, and revisions to contract documents.

❏ Requirements for a bid bond, if desired by the client.

❏ The form of bid and instructions that the bid form be filled out completely and properly signed. Bidders are expected to use the bid form exactly as presented.

Construction is generally bid on a lump sum basis for the complete project as defined in the contract documents. Additional costs requested may include alternates, allowances and bonding costs. Alternates are the costs to be added or deducted to the base bid if various identified alternate materials or systems are chosen. An allowance is a unit cost established for the supply of an item not yet selected. When the item is finally chosen and costed, the client receives a debit or credit as appropriate. Costs for bid bonds and other sureties are generally stated separately. If necessary, bidders may state other conditions or exceptions.

Bidding for furniture is generally more complicated. The bid form may be organized to include:

❏ A list of unit prices for each defined workplace, excluding tax. The price for each workplace will equal the total of unit prices for the workplace components.

❏ A summary showing the quantity of each workplace multiplied by its unit price resulting in the total cost per workplace type. These are added together to arrive at the total lump-sum price.

❏ A calculation showing the percentage reduction from list prices represented by the unit price bids.

❏ The time period during which unit prices remain effective, say, one to three years after the bid date.

❏ Prices for any alternates or allowances requested.

❏ Price increases that may take effect if work is performed on overtime.

❏ Storage charges if furniture installation is delayed for an extended time beyond the control of the furniture contractor.

Unlike construction, furniture is almost always bid on a unit price basis, since exact quantities and configurations are constantly changing, particularly for such large volume items as open plan workstations and workstation seating. The total lump-sum bid may be used to determine the low bidder on the project. The exact quantities stated on the purchase agreement will be priced according to the unit price schedules.

Unit prices often reflect quantity discounts and are therefore effective only within a certain quantity range for each item. Vendors may be asked to state the range within which unit prices apply and the adjustment that would be made if quantities exceed or fall below those amounts.

CONTRACT AGREEMENT

Contract documents for construction and furnishings include the drawings, specifications, general and supplementary conditions, a formal agreement, and various bonds and certificates.

The formal agreement may be a standard form, a purchase order, or an individualized contract prepared for the project. Standard contract forms include AIA and ASID document A171, "Standard Form of Agreement Between Owner and Contractor for Furniture, Furnishings, and Equipment." The agreement defines the parties to the contract, the work to be performed, the time of commencement and completion, and the payment to be received including amounts of retention and partial payment. It becomes operative when signed by both parties. One form of agreement is the preprinted purchase order usually prepared by a dealer or supplier. Often a bid is accepted by a client using a letter of intent. One or more purchase orders are then executed based on the bids and contract documents but only after final quantities have been determined and other details worked out.

Most purchase orders have contract conditions printed on the back. These conditions should be negotiable. They should be checked for discrepancies with the general conditions or other contract documents prepared by the architect or interior designer.

Many clients, particularly those with active facility management departments, use their own form of contract and have personnel devoted to managing the contracting process. Some large architecture and interior design firms have also prepared individualized forms of contract. As with any contract, the assistance of an attorney is recommended.

CHAPTER TWELVE

CONTRACT
ADMINISTRATION

When the drawings are completed and the contracts for construction and furnishings are signed, prime accountability for the project passes from the architect or interior designer to the construction and furnishings contractors. Under a direct contractual relationship with the client, they assume responsibility for implementing the project on time, on budget, and in accordance with the contract documents. The architect or interior designer is accountable during this phase of the work to monitor the project. He or she becomes the client's eyes and ears to see that the project is being produced as intended. The design team can advise, observe, and threaten, but primary control of the project is now out of its hands.

The tasks and authority of the architect or interior designer during the implementation phase of a project are defined in the professional service contract. They are also defined in the contracts for construction and furnishings and their general and supplementary conditions. The design professional's contract administration work described in the several sets of documents should be the same. An advantage of using standard AIA or ASID documents is the correlation between documents. If one standard form document is revised, related documents should be correspondingly modified for consistency.

The first duty of the contractor is to organize the project. This begins with orientation meetings during which the contractors describe the standard operating procedures they intend to use on the project. These may include schedule formats, site regulations, meeting agenda, submittal procedures, and many other processes necessary for the efficient prosecution of the project. To the extent that these agree with contract requirements, architects and interior designers should not object. Only when contrary to the intent of the contract should the architect or interior designer propose other procedures.

A prime contract is one between a

prime contractor and a client. Most office design projects have many prime contractors: a general contractor and a furnishings contractor plus the telephone company, moving company, and other suppliers of goods and services working directly for the client. When architectural woodworkers and carpet installers are under separate contract, they are considered prime contractors.

As the "first among equals" by virtue of the dollar amount of the contract as well as direct site responsibilities, the general construction contractor usually conducts job meetings, coordinates the work of other prime contractors as well as its own subcontractors, and prepares and maintains an overall progress schedule.

The job meeting is generally held weekly at the jobsite. This meeting is chaired by the general contractor who also prepares the agenda and minutes. The meeting should be attended by representatives of the client, the design firm, and, on an as-needed basis, other consultants, prime contractors, and subcontractors.

Contractor Coordination

Anytime there is coordination required between prime contractors on a project, a potential for problems exists. This may occur when construction, carpeting, and furniture installation overlaps in order to expedite move-in, when electrified open plan workstation panels must be installed by the general contractor's electricians, and when various suppliers of the client's computer or telecommunications equipment must have access to the site before occupancy. Although required by general conditions to cooperate with each other, prime contractors have no contractual relationship with each other and therefore no legal control. If the general construction contractor is unable or unwilling to provide this coordination, the client may look to the architect or interior designer for assistance.

Contractors are generally held responsible for damage to the work of others done by their crews. The general contractor may expect to be paid for repairing damage done by the carpet or furniture installers and a procedure should be in place to handle inspection, verification, and payment for this work.

On interiors projects, contractors are usually responsible for insuring that their product or service is compatible with the base building and agreeable to its management. Loading docks and elevators must be checked for size, capacity, and availability. Temporary storage or staging areas may be required. Noisy work may be prohibited during normal business hours when other building tenants might be disturbed. Access to other tenant spaces may need to be arranged for installation of electrical or other work.

Progress Schedule

Prime contractors are obligated to provide the client with detailed progress schedules of their work. These schedules should show relationships between subcontractors and suppliers, and dates of ordering, submittals, manufacture, construction, transportation, and installation. These are successful only if the information is accurate, if the format is easily understood, and if they are updated regularly. When appropriate, these schedules should be verified by factory acknowledgments and other confirmations.

Most large general contracting firms and furniture dealers and manufacturers have sophisticated computerized critical path scheduling systems. An advantage of these systems is their ability to identify critical activities and spot potential problems. Their disadvantage is that they may contain too much information for the client's needs and be too cumbersome and expensive to reissue frequently.

Submittals

During the course of construction the contractor is generally required to make numerous submittals for review by the architect, interior designer, or engineers. These may include shop drawings for such items as millwork and mechanical ductwork, schedules for doors, frames, hardware, and finishes, cut sheets of manufactured items such as light fixtures and plumbing fixtures, and samples of paint colors and finishes. The submittal requirements are defined in the contract specifications.

Submittals are prepared by subcontractors using the contract documents and, when necessary, field measurements. These submittals are the final document used in the selection or construction of the item in question and as such must be absolutely accurate. Submittals are given by the subcontractor to the general contractor or construction manager, who should check them thoroughly before submission to the design firm.

The architect or interior designer must carefully check every line, word, and number on the submittal. Generally there is a choice of three actions that may be taken. When there are no corrections, the architect or interior designer approves the submittal and allows the work to proceed. If there are only minor corrections, the design professional may allow the work to proceed in accordance with these corrections. In such cases corrected documents may be submitted after the fact for record purposes. If the submittal is seriously incorrect or incomplete, the architect or interior designer may ask that it be revised and resubmitted before work proceeds.

A basic principal of construction is that architects and interior designers determine *what* is to be produced while contractors are responsible for *how* work is to be accomplished. Standard AIA and ASID documents contain wording relieving the design firm from responsibility for "means, methods, and techniques" for the work. Consequently the checking of submittals by the design firm is for "conformance with the design concept" only. In practice, the design professional should be sure that he or she understands and agrees with everything presented in the submittal. Without questioning the contractors' prerogatives, the design professional should thoroughly understand the "means, methods, and techniques" proposed for the project. When problems arise, the design professional is likely to be blamed, regardless of what the contract says.

The architect or interior designer needs to be given sufficient time for submittal review. Construction and furnishings contracts typically allow ten days. Contractors should schedule submittal preparation and review so that they occur early enough to allow for changes and revisions, if necessary, and so that they arrive in an orderly fashion—not all at once.

Substitutions

After contracts have been executed, substitutions of materials or furnishings for those specified should be discouraged. The general requirements, division 1 of the specifications, will usually state the conditions under which the client will consider substitutions proposed by contractors. First, the contractor must have a good reason, such as the fact that the specified product is no longer available or would take too long to obtain. Second, the cost and quality of the proposed substitute product must be equal to that specified. (There can be no question of the contractor making additional profit by proposing a substitute.)

Substitutions can have a domino effect. A different material or furniture piece can affect many other selections. Extensive review and analysis of contractor-proposed substitute materials, furnishings, or systems may be justification for additional fees for the architect or interior designer.

The Management of Change

Change is inevitable. Even on projects where the design was frozen sometime during design development, there will be changes during construction. These are caused by many things: the drawings are not perfect, site conditions vary from what was expected, cost or time saving opportunities are discovered, or the client sees desirable revisions or additions to the project.

From whatever the source, changes must be smoothly integrated into the overall flow of work.

The management of the change process should be thoroughly discussed at the initiation of construction. Even though changes are defined in detail in the contracts for construction or furnishings and the general conditions, most contractors and design firms and many clients have their own favorite methods and procedures.

Before a change can be implemented it must be identified and documented, its impact on cost, schedule, and fees determined, and it must be approved by the client and contractor. A change may be initiated by anyone, client, contractor, or design team, but it is usually the design firm's field representative who initiates the paperwork. This usually takes the form of a *bulletin* or request for change document. The bulletin describes

the change in detail, including drawings and specifications as necessary, and asks the contractor to prepare a cost proposal and to assess the schedule impact by a stated date.

The bulletin should also state who requested the change and the reason for the change. It's important to record this information at the beginning of the process to simplify the resolution of disagreements or the placing of blame later on.

If extensive drawings are involved in the change, there may be additional fees due the design firm or engineers. If it is likely that the change may not be implemented, the contractor may be asked to prepare estimates based on a brief description of the work rather than complete drawings. Based on these estimates the client may then authorize the consultant to prepare full documentation for additional fees.

The contract for construction or furnishings or the general conditions outlines the methods to be used in preparing estimates for changes. These documents specify the records to be kept, when unit prices are applicable, allowable amounts for overhead and fees, and other conditions applicable to change orders. Once the contractor has identified the cost and schedule impact, the architect or interior designer prepares a *change order* for the client's approval. The design professional processes the paperwork but almost never has authority to actually approve change orders. Upon approval by the client and acceptance by the contractor, the work proceeds.

A cardinal principle of construction is that no change can be implemented unless approved in writing. This necessitates a lot of paperwork, which in itself takes time, often more time than can be allowed if the change is to be implemented efficiently. Many changes occur on

BULLETIN

To: C. C. Baxter/General Contractor

Project: Federal Broadcasting/Records Department Remodeling

Date: July 16, 19—

We intend to amend the contract documents as follows. Please submit a written quotation of changes in cost and time, if any, for each item. Do not proceed with work on these revisions until a change order has been approved.

8A2   Ceiling Plan/Floor 8   Rev. 1   7/15/—

Relocate 4 downlights as shown because of restricted beam clearance.

8A3   Outlet Plan/Floor 8   Rev. 3   7/15/—

General revisions owing to revisions in computer requirements.

8A4   Finishes Plan/Floor 8   Rev. 2   7/15/—

Revise wall finish W2 in room 807 to W3 as requested by owner.

Revise wall finish P1 in room 816 to P3 as requested by owner.

8A6   Elevations/Floor 8   Rev. 1   7/15/—

Clarification of mirror height in room 812.

Wall finish revisions as noted above.

Clarification of clock outlet mounting height in room 815.

By: Jed Leland

CC: Bunny Watson/Federal Broadcasting
       Richard Sumner/Federal Broadcasting

BULLETIN. A bulletin may be used to make clarifications or request pricing for revisions. However, the actual authorization for change is the change order.

projects that demand immediate approval. One method to accomplish these urgent changes is by the use of a *field order*. This is a one-page form that contains all the information required in a change order but is designed to be filled in on the spot by the contractor's and design firm's representatives in the field. The client's signed approval is still required. For accounting purposes, field orders may be periodically combined into a formal change order.

Usually the only changes to the work that the architect or interior designer may unilaterally authorize are those that have no impact on cost or time and that are consistent with the intent of the contract documents.

Punch List

When work has progressed to the point that the client can beneficially occupy the new offices, the contractor informs the architect or interior designer that the project is substantially complete. The design professional and the engineers then prepare *punch lists*. This is a formal, room-by-room listing of all items not yet complete, installed incorrectly, or in need of repair before the project can be considered acceptable. A punch list should be specific, stating exactly what is at fault. Punch lists should never be used to effect changes in the work. A punch list should tell the contractor *what* is wrong, not attempt to tell the contractor *how* to make the correction. Separate punch lists should be prepared for each prime contractor on the project but should not attempt to identify the subcontractor responsible. Upon receipt of the punch lists the prime contractors will make those determinations and distribute copies of the list to the appropriate subcontractors.

The design firm or engineers may refuse to prepare a punch list if the work is obviously not complete. Punch lists should not be used as progress reviews.

After receipt of the punch lists the contractors should complete work within a few days or weeks. Punch list work should not be allowed to drag on for months. When all corrective work is complete, the architect or interior designer and engineers again review the work, punch list in hand, and cross-out those items that have been satisfactorily completed. If items remain, the punch list is returned to the contractor. If, at the beginning of the review, it is obvious that little punch list work has been accomplished, the design professional or engineer can refuse to continue the inspection.

A punch list is primarily for the convenience of contractors. It is not a definitive document and does not relieve the contractor from performing remedial work that may not be listed.

Clients may also prepare lists of items they believe need completion or correction. These should be edited by design professionals and integrated with their own lists.

Punch lists may also be prepared at times when certain responsibilities are being transferred from one prime contractor to another. A typical instance is when the carpet contractor begins work. Representatives of the general contractor, carpet contractor, and design firm may tour the project identifying any damage or touch-up that is the responsibility of the general contractor. After carpet installation, the project is again reviewed and any new damage to general construction work is then presumed to be the responsibility of the carpet contractor. This is generally minor and the two prime contractors usually can work out an arrangement for making the repairs. In serious cases the general contractor

PUNCH LIST

To: C. C. Baxter/General Contractor

Project: Federal Broadcasting/Records Department Remodeling

Date: August 16, 19—

We have observed the following deficiencies requiring corrective action:

All Spaces

    1. Install all permanent thermostats.

    2. Clean white chalk marks from resilient base.

Room 401

    1. Add base at reception counter.

    2. Poor seaming at wall fabric on south wall.

    3. Clean glass entry doors.

Room 402

    1. Ceiling misalignment in southeast corner.

    2. Paint splattering at column 3H.

    3. Replace missing light fixture lens.

Room 403

    1. Misaligned outlet cover plate.

    2. Touch-up north wall.

    3. Remove tape from door jamb.

By: Jed Leland

CC: Bunny Watson/Federal Broadcasting
            Richard Sumner/Federal Broadcasting

PUNCH LIST. This is a list of deficiencies that the contractor must correct before the project can be considered complete.

may charge the owner, who then must deduct a like amount from the carpet contractor's payment.

OCCUPANCY

Preparation for an office move and the move itself requires careful planning. The responsibility is primarily the client's; few professional service contracts require much more than vague assistance from the architect or interior designer. For large projects the services of a relocation consultant may be useful; for small projects the responsibility usually falls on the client's office manager.

As a general principle, furniture and paper not needed in the new offices should not be moved. For disposal of existing furniture there are several options. Clients with an active corporate standards program may be able to return some of the furniture to inventory to be stored for use on a future project. The furniture dealer who will supply the bulk of the new furniture for the project may be willing to dispose of the old. Used furniture is generally worth very little, but there are companies that may be willing to purchase used office furniture for refurbishment and resale to other organizations. Finally, used furniture may be donated to charity; the client's tax advisor should be consulted for potential tax benefits, if any.

An office move is an opportunity to implement a paper purge campaign. It is not unusual for well over 50 percent of an organization's files to be useless; either out-of-date, unnecessary duplications, not identifiable, mislabeled, or misfiled. Many files may serve no practical purpose other than to fulfill legal file retention requirements and may be more economically stored in a less expensive remote location.

Filing space and furniture requirements are usually established during the programming phase of the project with a paper purge campaign in mind, and unless the campaign is implemented, the new facilities may be inadequate.

An effective paper purge campaign requires organization and commitment. A definition of what may or should be disposed of must be established. Employees will need encouragement and an orientation to the process. Most difficult, management must allocate time for what they will probably consider to be nonproductive activity.

Moving consultants or relocation management consultants may assist in the inventory of existing furnishings, assist in the disposal of existing non-reuse items, develop records purge campaigns, schedule and otherwise manage phased moves to new quarters, prepare budgets for the move, and assist in the selection of a moving company and oversee their work.

A moving company must be selected. It will be responsible for tagging existing furniture, equipment, and other material, developing a move schedule, coordination with building management for loading dock and elevator access, performing the move itself, clean up, and resolution of any damage claims. Unlike other contractors, moving contractors generally work on an hourly basis. Although estimated costs and not-to-exceed bids may be given, the final cost will depend on the actual volume of material moved. Selection of a moving company is generally made on the basis of reputation, references, and a convincing presentation of services to be provided.

The success of an office move often hinges on an employee orientation program. Some employees naturally resist change, no matter how beneficial. Some employees may feel ignored, others that their new workplaces will be inadequate, and still others that the new location is inconvenient. These attitudes can cause serious morale problems. An orientation program both before and after the move can do much to alleviate these problems.

Before the move, employees should be made to feel that they are fully informed, that their wishes have been considered, and that they are part of the process. Group meetings and presentations, question and answer sessions, and newsletters may be effective.

Tours of the new offices during construction are good morale boosters; however, these should always be guided tours coordinated by the general contractor. Under no circumstances should the client's employees be allowed on the jobsite unescorted. In addition to the physical danger, employees may attempt to ask questions or give direction to construction workers, thus causing serious contractual problems.

Employee orientation should include instruction in the use of new furnishings and equipment. Ergonomic chairs, in particular, have become complex mechanisms that require explanation if employees are to take full advantage of the various adjustability features.

During the move itself, the client should establish a policy concerning employee participation. In most cases too many people present during the move causes confusion. On the other hand, employees may be invited to come in on a Sunday to "get organized" before the Monday workday.

After the move there will be inevitable complaints ranging from incomplete construction to lost furniture to equipment improperly installed. To minimize frustration, a formal procedure should be established. Generally employees should

be asked to make their comments in writing to a designated individual, usually the office manager, with an assurance that the problem will be addressed within a given time frame. Genuine emergencies should be taken care of immediately; solutions to most complaints can wait several days.

As-Built Documents

As-built drawings are a record of exactly what was constructed or installed on a project. For office projects they usually consist of a set of contract documents marked up to show field changes. Their preparation is generally the responsibility of the contractors.

As-built documents are useful for large or complex projects and on projects undergoing constant revision and reconfiguration. If the project was produced on CADD, the client may be willing to contract with the architect or interior designer to enter as-built information into the CADD system, to maintain a CADD data base of project revisions, or to assist the client's facility management staff in the utilization of CADD for project maintenance, property management, and strategic planning.

Project Photography

Projects with potential for publication or business development should be professionally photographed shortly after occupancy. The architect or interior designer should hire the best photographer he or she can afford; the quality of the photographs must be the equal of the quality of the project when magazine editors select projects for publication.

The architect or interior designer should be present and specify which views should be shot. The photographer will also have suggestions. Photography generally takes place on weekends or after business hours. The premises should be thoroughly cleaned and all papers and other clutter moved out of sight. Good photography takes time; four to eight shots in a day is reasonable.

For a variety of reasons, some clients are reluctant to have their office space publicized, and they should always be asked for permission for photography and publication.

Project Close-out

After client work on a project has been concluded, there still remains one more task for the architect or interior designer—project close-out. Project close-out may include:

❏ Organizing files and documents, discarding duplicates, and preparing the balance for dead filing.

❏ Preparing a project history and other statistical information about fees, costs, and schedules for marketing purposes and as a reference for future projects.

❏ An evaluation of the project in terms of quality and efficiency and an evaluation of the performance of consultants and contractors for in-house reference.

This is often the most neglected part of the project. The work is generally not billable and everyone is anxious to move on to the next project. If not done, however, the project loses much of its value as a base of experience for future projects, wastes inordinate amounts of time in searching for documents and informa-tion when questions arise in the future, and wastes valuable space storing unnecessary files and prints.

FOLLOW UP

A completed project should not be forgotten. Contact should be maintained with the client and the project should be visited periodically to be sure that everything is going smoothly. There will be minor revisions over the life of the project that the architect and interior designer should be willing to do.

The office design process has now come full circle. A satisfied client is the best reference for new work. The client may have additional projects or need facility management services. They may have business associates or friends who need design services.

A post-occupancy evaluation, occurring six months to a year after move-in, may have benefits for both the client and the design professional. This evaluation may consist of a meeting between the client and the project team to review design and functional goals to see how well they were met, to evaluate the suitability and durability of construction and furnishings, and to identify areas where modifications are required. Architects and interior designers may be reluctant to conduct post-occupancy evaluations because of fears of negative criticism. It is usually better, however, to confront such criticism directly and correct the problems. Clients appreciate an ongoing interest in their projects, and this can contribute to successful long-term business relationships.

AFTERWORD

The quarter century ending with the nineties brought a revolution in the office. White-collar workers, formerly considered as back office support for manufacturing, have taken center stage in an age of information. Computers, which began this period as the province of highly trained specialists in isolated departments, are now ubiquitous, with a terminal located on virtually every desk. Office furnishings, once limited to a choice between highly styled wood and gray or khaki metal pieces, are now available in sophisticated systems with infinite componentry and close integration with computer and telecommunications equipment. Design, once done by the office manager on graph paper, is now performed by experienced and talented architects and interior designers.

These advances have made the modern office a splendid place to work. All of the problems have not been solved, however. There are still many questions to challenge the owners, managers, designers, and builders of office space in the years ahead.

Where is the computer taking the office worker?
Computerization seems to be heading in two diverse directions. One direction is toward increased creativity, limited only by the imagination. Computers have enormous potential for opening new areas for human endeavor.

The computer's very potential to simplify and automate processes, however,

has resulted in millions of clerks playing "fill in the blanks" without even the relief of hitting a carriage return or changing a typewriter ribbon. This mindless, repetitive work, so like the worst features of the industrial assembly line, is resulting in severe physical and psychological problems in the white-collar work force.

Perhaps this aspect of computerization is a temporary phase; as automation develops, the need for this mindless input will become less and less. Noncreative clerical positions will be phased out, and the office will be populated solely with highly educated, motivated thinkers and decision makers.

Which leads to another problem. What will become of all those office workers, poorly trained by a deteriorating school system and unable to master the creative side of computing, who will be faced with diminishing job opportunities?

How productive is the office?

Industrial assembly line work is measured by the number of units produced during a given time, modified by the number of errors. Measuring office work in this way has been disappointing, and those who measure such things have been complaining for years about the woeful state of office productivity.

For many workers, quantitative productivity measurement poses a threat. With the computer, it is simple to measure output. A supervisor no longer has to hover over workers, exhorting them to work faster. The computer can provide a print-out showing the exact production of each worker down to the last digit. This can be intimidating, and some workers are complaining that the Big Brother of Orwell's *1984* is a frightening reality.

Perhaps we are measuring the wrong things. Perhaps office work should somehow be evaluated in terms of quality rather than quantity. Shouldn't workers be judged not on the number of decisions made during the day or on the volume of paper produced but on the quality of those decisions and the excellence of those papers?

How dangerous is the office?

Each month seems to bring new threats. First it was asbestos, then the sick building syndrome, and now repetitive strain injuries. Worker health and safety has emerged as a major issue, and there is increasing pressure to improve the working environment.

Health and safety problems pose the threat of litigation not only for employers but for architects and interior designers as well. The concept of professional service with all of its subjectivity and risk of error is being challenged by a business orientation that demands absolute objectivity and perfection. Society seems unable to tolerate mistakes in opinion or invention and is willing to sue when this occurs. This results not only in dramatically increasing costs for liability insurance but increasing timidity on the part of design professionals and pressure to avoid taking responsibility and to stick with the tried and true.

Is office design an art or a science?

It is an article of faith among architects and interior designers that each combination of site, program, and corporate culture demands creativity and a unique result for the project. This is being questioned by some who believe that office design ends at space planning; that open plan workstations can be simply and successfully arranged by computer, the modern equivalent of the office manager armed with graph paper. Like most things, the truth is probably somewhere in between and depends on the project. Operational office space relying on a well-developed corporate standards program requires a different design approach from the highly individualized law office or corporate executive suite.

A key factor in this discussion may be the role of CADD. Computer-aided design and drafting is universally accepted as a method for production of contract documents. Not so well accepted is its role in design. This may, however, ultimately be its most important role. Design on computer is not a matter of simply moving the soft pencil and yellow tracing paper onto the computer screen, but has the potential for a new approach to design. Where ten or twenty variations of a given concept or detail could be studied manually, hundreds can be analyzed quickly by computer. More important, perhaps, is the encouragement the computer gives to modular, systematic, and logical thinking.

Who will design the office?
First, there is the question of licensing. Architects and interior designers are engaged in a heated debate over their respective competencies. The issues are complicated and being fought out in the legislatures of the various states where proposals for the licensing of interior designers are being introduced.

Then there is the role of the facility manager. Facility management as an organized profession is still young and still undefined in many areas. There are signs, however, of increasing involvement in the office planning and design process at the expense of the traditional roles of architects and interior designers. Many companies are moving the planning and design function in-house. There is little question that the management of corporate facilities is necessary and valuable, however, the full implications for design professionals as well as the ramifications for the design of the office itself are still unclear.

Still others want to be involved in office planning and design and their roles are equally undefined. There are many players in the game. Some furniture dealers and manufacturers provide space planning and design services, and even accounting firms and management consultants are showing interest in the field. Ultimately there will be a place for everybody; what that place will be is an evolving issue.

What will the office of the future be like?
The office of the future will not be a slick, paperless spaceship control room. It will be a working, living environment, perhaps messy, but totally responsive to the needs of the people who inhabit it. It will be a challenge to architects and interior designers to understand and create such a place.

BIBLIOGRAPHY

American Institute of Architects and American Society of Interior Designers. Document A171: "Standard Form of Agreement Between Owner and Contractor for Furniture, Furnishings, and Equipment"; Document A177: "Abbreviated Form of Agreement Between Owner and Contractor for Furniture, Furnishings, and Equipment"; Document A271: "General Conditions of the Contract for Furniture, Furnishings and Equipment"; Document A771: "Instructions to Interiors Bidders"; Document B171: "Standard Form of Agreement for Interior Design Services"; Document B177: "Abbreviated Form of Agreement for Interior Design Services."

Architectural Woodwork Quality Standards, Guide Specifications, and Quality Certification Program. Arlington, Va.: Architectural Woodwork Institute, 1985.

Bailey, Stephen. *Offices.* London: Butterworth Architecture, 1990.

Becker, Franklin. *The Total Workplace.* New York: Van Nostrand Reinhold, 1990.

Binder, Stephen. *Corporate Facility Planning.* New York: McGraw-Hill, 1989.

Bramwell, M., ed. *The International Book of Wood.* New York: Simon and Schuster, 1976.

Brill, Michael, with Stephen T. Margulis, Ellen Konar, and the Buffalo Organization for Social and Technological Innovation (BOSTI). *Using Office Design To Increase Productivity.* 2 vols. Buffalo: Workplace Design and Productivity, 1984.

Callender, J. H., ed. *Time-Saver Standards for Architectural Design Data.* New York: McGraw-Hill, 1982.

Chedd, G. *Sound.* Garden City, N.Y.: Doubleday, 1970.

Curtis, Jack. *Taking the Guesswork Out of Office Acoustics.* Cambridge: BBN Laboratories, 1979.

Fire Resistance Design Data Manual. Chicago: Gypsum Association, 1973.

Friedmann, A., J. F. Pile, and F. Wilson. *Interior Design: An Introduction to Architectural Interiors.* New York: Elsevier, 1982.

Gypsum Construction Handbook. Chicago: United States Gypsum Company, 1980.

Harris, David A., Alvin E. Palmer, M. Susan Lewis, David L. Munson, Gershon Meckler, and Ralph Gerdes. *Planning and Designing the Office Environment.* New York: Van Nostrand Reinhold, 1981.

Hoke J. R., Jr., ed. *Architectural Graphic Standards*. New York: John Wiley & Sons, 1988.

Hornbostel, C., and W. J. Hornung. *Materials and Methods for Contemporary Construction*. Englewood Cliffs, N.J.: Prentice-Hall, 1982.

Jones, Gerre. *How to Market Professional Design Services*. New York: McGraw-Hill, 1983.

Klein, Judy Graf. *The Office Book*. New York: Facts on File, 1982.

Pile, John. *Open Office Planning*. New York: Whitney Library of Design, 1978.

Pile, J. F. *Interior Design*. New York: Harry N. Abrams, 1988.

Probst, Robert. *The Office: A Facility Based on Change*. Zeeland, Mich.: Herman Miller, 1968.

Pulgram, William L., and Richard E. Stonis. *Designing the Automated Office*. New York: Whitney Library of Design, 1984.

Reznikoff, S. C. *Interior Graphic and Design Standards*. New York: Whitney Library of Design, 1986.

Riggs, J. R. *Materials and Components of Interior Design*. Englewood Cliffs, N.J.: Prentice-Hall, Inc., 1989.

Rupp, W., with A. Friedmann. *Construction Materials for Interior Design*. New York: Whitney Library of Design, 1989.

Saphier, Michael. *Office Planning and Design*. New York: McGraw-Hill, 1968.

Saphier, Michael. *Planning the New Office*. New York: McGraw-Hill, 1978.

Shoshkes, Lila. *Space Planning*. New York: Architectural Record Books, 1976.

Uniform Building Code. Whittier, Ca.: International Conference of Building Officials, 1988.

Watson, D. *Construction Materials and Processes*. New York: McGraw-Hill, 1986.

INDEX

STALLS
TYP. PUBLIC
32" x 56"
HANDI
36" x 5'5"

MIN. EXITS
0-500   2
500-1,000   3
1,000 +   4

EXIT STAIRWAY PASSAGES
MUST BE FIRE
CONST.   1hr — 1-4 FLOORS
      2hr — 5+ FLOORS

(NEVAMAR LAM)

SMALL ASSEM (50)
CLASS RM. (20)
OFFICES (30)

EXIT DOORS 3' +
OPEN OUT

NO EXIT 150' FROM
ANOTHER + NO ONE
PERSON MORE THAN 150'
            AWAY
DEAD END CORRIDORS
NO MORE THAN 20'

AUDITORIUMS
14 SEATS BETWEEN AISLE
7 IF ONLY ONE AISLE

MIN. 44" / EXIT

2 WAYS

3 GOALS OF FIRE
           CODES
1) PROTECT OCCUPANTS
2) HELP FIGHTERS
WHEN FIGHTING
FIRES
3) HELP BUILDING
SURVIVE FIRE

The predicted path of Halley's Comet during its 1985-6 return.

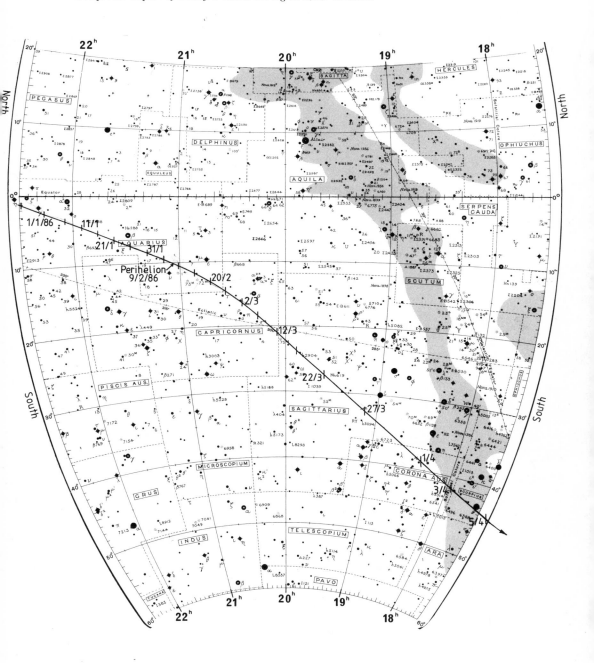